ABOLITION
AND THE
UNDERGROUND
RAILROAD
in
SOUTH JERSEY

Not Without a Fight

Ellen D. Alford

THE
History
PRESS

Published by The History Press
Charleston, SC
www.historypress.com

First published 2023

Manufactured in the United States

ISBN 9781467155199

Library of Congress Control Number: 2023938400

To my parents, Lighty and Daisy Mae, for life and love of family, and special appreciation to my mother for introducing me to the importance of the Underground Railroad and the Civil War. Also, I thank my brother, my sisters and Aunt Virginia for their immense support and love.

CONTENTS

CONTENTS

PREFACE

This is a most brave place; whatever envy or evil spies may speak of it,
I could wish you all here.
—Colonial writer John Crips, from Burlington Story

There are still stories to be told about abolition and the Underground Railroad (UGRR) in South Jersey. Although much has been written about the UGRR, more can be done to research and write about this courageous effort in South Jersey. The fact that we know so little about abolitionist Harriet Tubman's activity in the region speaks to not only her expertise as an UGRR conductor but also historians' need to do more investigation. This same thought applies to the Black Civil War soldiers from South Jersey who have been overlooked in the history books. This book in no way pretends to answer all the questions, but I believe it will add to the conversation about abolition and the UGRR in South Jersey and, hopefully, aid further research or at least change how people think about the part this region played in that drama statewide and nationally.

ACKNOWLEDGEMENTS

This project would not have been possible without the support of my friends and neighbors, Janice and Colonel Joseph Murray, Marietta and Leroy Webster, Diane and Greg Lilley, Vivian Guyton, Linda Casmer, Joann Lucas, Norma Stockton and Carmen Pagan as well as information from governmental agencies, historical societies, libraries and institutions offered through the professional courtesies of staff at the National Archives, Library of Congress, New Jersey State Library, New Jersey State Archives, National Park Service and U.S. Bureau of the Census.

Further information was obtained from the Gloucester County Historical Society; Camden County Historical Society; Salem County Historical Society; Cape May County Historical & Genealogical Society; Salem Quarterly Meeting (Quaker); Bethel Othello AME Church, Springtown; Mount Zion AME Church, Swedesboro; Macedonia AME Church, Camden; Bethel AME Church, Woodbury; Harriet Tubman Museum, Cape May; Harriet Tubman Home, Auburn, New York; Seward House, Auburn, New York; Mid-Atlantic Center for the Arts, Cape May; Peter Mott House; Swedesboro Economic Development Committee; New Bedford Whaling Museum, Massachusetts; American Colonization Society; GPS coordinates; New Jersey Colonization Society; OhioHistoryCentral.org; the Union League, Philadelphia; University of Pennsylvania, Van Pelt/Dietrich Library; the Second New Jersey Brigade, New Jersey's Civil War Brigade Re-enactors; InternetArchive.org; Betty Bajewicz Historical Center, Franklin

Township, Gloucester County; Gloucester County Courthouse, New Jersey; and Vineland Historical and Antiquarian Society.

My sincerest gratitude for invaluable consultation offered by project readers: Joseph G. Bilby, author of *"Freedom to All": New Jersey's African American Civil War Soldiers;* Robert Bowell, captain of the Twenty-Second Regiment USCT reenacting organization, Second New Jersey Brigade; Dennis Rizzo, author of *Parallel Communities: The Underground Railroad in South Jersey*; Lieutenant Colonel Joseph Winfield Murray II, U.S. Army Signal Corps (retired); Major Joseph Winfield Murray III, U.S. Quartermaster Corps (active duty); and Jennifer Parisi, Newfield library staff.

My most gracious thanks go out to all the librarians who have assisted me in my research and obtained even hard-to-find materials and books or directed me to where I could find necessary reference materials, especially those at Newfield Public Library, including: Carol Thomasson, current director; Carol Baughman and Susan Mounier, past directors; and present and past staff members Bonnie Patterson, Jennifer Parisi, Marina Boesz, Alice Distefano, Mary Mikula, Theresa Mikula and Leo Warner. Also, my appreciation goes out to the Gloucester County Library Consortium; Franklin Township Public Library; Cape May County Library; Rutgers University Paul Robson Library, Camden; Barbara Price, Gloucester County Historical Society; Richard J. Guido Jr., Salem County Historical Society; Carol J. Coulbourn, Betty Bajewicz Historical Center; James G. Mundy Jr. and Keeley Tulio, Union League Library, Philadelphia; Patricia A. Martinelli, Vineland Historical and Antiquarian Society; and Dr. Howard Gillette Jr., professor emeritus, History Department, Rutgers University, Camden, for his support.

Lastly, my deepest appreciation is given to the Quakers and abolitionists of South Jersey, Harriet Tubman and the soldiers of the Twenty-Second Regiment United States Colored Troops (USCT) for their sacrifice and hard work for freedom.

CHAPTER 1

PRELUDE TO A WAR

Salt of the earth": that's what people say about others who exemplify qualities or behaviors that are worthy of being imitated or modeled. Salt is a very versatile and important substance. It can season food or make it inedible. It can purify or corrode. Mixed with water, it can be used to heal, but added to other compounds, it can be explosive. Rooted in the marl-rich, fertile, sometimes sandy soil of the southern half of the Garden State lived a "salt of the earth" people destined to become fierce warriors for a race and defenders of a nation that denied some liberty and citizenship. For these people, Quakers and free Blacks, abolition became their tool and method of defiance against injustice after the Revolutionary War and throughout the antebellum period up to the Civil War. Their defiant stance and support created an atmosphere where abolitionists could work to end slavery and fostered a boldness that seeped into the inner core of Black residents across South Jersey. Although Quakers held to a doctrine of nonviolence and opposed war, those in West Jersey developed a special antithesis to slavery that morphed into devotion for liberty toward the bonded.

This brazen spirit also affected Black men across the region, leading to the acclaimed fighting spirit of those who joined the Twenty-Second Regiment United States Colored Troops (USCT) during the Civil War. The Twenty-Second was one of the most highly regarded colored regiments during the war and was made up mostly by New Jersey men. These soldiers were acclaimed for their bravery and selected over other colored regiments for specific service after Lincoln was assassinated. Together, Quakers and Blacks contended against the "peculiar institution" and vied for liberty.

QUAKER RALLY

The desire to emancipate slaves in South Jersey began before the War for Independence with Quaker leaders, such as George Fox and John Woolman, preaching to other members of the Society of Friends. In 1652, Fox excitedly told a large crowd of people in England about his own spiritual revelation that everyone has within themselves the ability to experience God and, in turn, respond to his presence. Fox contended that intermediaries were not needed to communicate with God and that religious authority was not reserved just for a select few. This was the beginning of a new religion that spread quickly in England, converting many, although not without opposition from the Church of England and the English government.[1] In 1672, Fox brought his religious ideology to America on a visit to East Jersey.[2]

When the English took control of New Amsterdam in the New World, forcing the Dutch out, in 1664, King Charles II granted a proprietary land charter of New Jersey to his brother, James, the Duke of York. The duke then divided the proprietary rights to the colony between two Cavaliers loyal to the crown: John, Lord Berkeley, and Sir George Carteret. Sir Carteret was awarded land between the Delaware and Hudson Rivers in East Jersey (present-day North Jersey) and John, Lord Berkeley, was awarded land in West Jersey (present-day South Jersey). However, both Berkeley and Carteret lost their rights to the lands in 1673 when the Dutch recaptured New York and all English holdings in the region. The following year, the English regained control over the territory; however, by that time, Lord Berkeley had sold his half of New Jersey to Quakers Edward Byllynge and John Fenwick in 1673, perhaps without realizing he had lost the rights. When Lord Berkeley offered his American holdings for sale, Fenwick saw an opportunity to escape the oppression he and other Quakers were facing in England and co-purchased the land along with Byllynge.[3] Confusion arose over the land transfer, and it took until 1675 for the situation to be resolved, with the Byllynge holdings converted to three Quaker trustees: William Penn, Nicolas Lucas and Gawen Lawrie. The trustees then divided the holdings into one hundred shares, with ten shares going to Fenwick and the remaining held in trust to pay off Byllynge's bankruptcy debts. Fenwick's portion was one-tenth of the land in West Jersey, comprising all of present-day Salem and Cumberland Counties.

In 1676, the trustees adopted a document that served as a constitution for West Jersey called "The Concessions and Agreements of the Proprietors, Freeholders and Inhabitants of the Province of West Jersey in America." This document gave West Jersey settlers seventy acres of land; those who

Dividing line for East and West Jersey, 1676 map. (Sources: Wright, *Afro-Americans in New Jersey* and Lundin, *Cockpit of the Revolution*.) *Author's drawing.*

arrived with servants or slaves would receive an additional seventy acres. This was for the year 1677, but in subsequent years, settlers also obtained additional lands of a lesser amount if they arrived with servants or slaves. This benefit was an incentive for Englishmen and women who had financial means to purchase land and immigrate to the province. But it also served as encouragement to those settlers to acquire slaves. The "Concessions" made it clear that settlers "inhabiting the said Province shall as farr [sic] as in us lies be free from oppression and slavery." That same year, the province of New Jersey was divided into East and West.[4] Evidently, the freedom expressed was only meant for Europeans.

Once the problem with the Byllynge holding was resolved, William Penn encouraged other Quakers to purchase land in West Jersey so they could form their own societies. Fenwick also had the same idea, and prior to Penn's pronouncement, Fenwick brought a group of settlers, including his family and servants, to his Salem colony in October 1675. This was the first English colony on the Delaware River. In August 1677, 230 other Quakers accepted Penn's offer, arriving in West Jersey near Raccoon Creek (present-day Swedesboro) with their household goods. Over the years, more Quaker settlers arrived across the region and established themselves in positions of authority and influence. The Byllynge holdings eventually were sold and resold, ending up in the hands of the West Jersey Society, run by a group of forty-eight men in London. This ended the total control of West Jersey by Quakers, since Englishmen of the Anglican faith began moving into the area. However, Quakers were still able to maintain a degree of authority as well as solidity and peace in their regular lives through their religion and by forming worship groups in individual homes and, subsequently, building meetinghouses. Because of their start in the areas along the Delaware River, the West Jersey Quakers "retained a cultural flavor that was different from East Jersey," argued Richard McCormick.[5] But just as in East Jersey, slavery was encouraged both by landowners and the constitution. In West Jersey, the "Concessions and Agreements" not only appointed additional lands to settlers who arrived with servants or slaves but also prohibited ship captains from transporting any person without a certificate and established regulations concerning chattel.[6]

Pacifist, Not Passionless

Although slavery was sanctioned by colonial society, some Quakers began to question its justification and morality. Believing God made all men equal, they were the first group to register a protest against the institution in America. As a result, in 1679, Fox urged his followers to begin teaching Blacks and Indians to read so they could get a religious education. In the late 1600s, the Church of England required that slaves who converted to Christianity be manumitted by their owners. Later, the bishop of London established a new statute declaring conversion by slaves did not require manumission. Despite the fact that this new statute permitted some education for some slaves, it mainly acted to relieve slave owners from the fear that teaching their chattel to read and write would release them from their enslavement. Now Africans could be converted to Christianity as a way to civilize them with no fear to slave owners. As a result, some Anglican churches offered to convert and teach slaves to read, but the Quakers offered slaves their best chance for manumission, even though they did not accept Black membership.[7] For Quakers, teaching their slaves to read and write was only the beginning of the changes that would affect the enslaved. Starting in 1684, the New Jersey and Pennsylvania Quaker meetings began sending delegates to the Yearly Meeting held alternately in Philadelphia and Burlington, New Jersey. The Yearly Meeting was the governing body that settled all problems and business arising from the Monthly Meetings. Four years later, the Germantown Mennonites recorded an antislavery protest in their Annual Meeting, which also included the New Jersey sect of Friends' Annual Meeting. Their statement asserted that slavery was in opposition to Christian teachings, responsible for destroying Black families and cruel. They blamed slave traders, kidnappers and owners for this evil. The protest also pointed out that Quakers could not claim they stood for liberty if they kept slaves themselves. Other Quakers then began to speak out against slavery. George Keith wrote an "Exhortation" in 1693 criticizing slave owners for their greed and called on Quakers to free their slaves.[8]

But Burlington County Quaker John Woolman had a stronger, more influential presence in New Jersey and across the colonies, preaching and teaching the gospel while strongly urging manumission. In 1746, Woolman and a companion from the Society of Friends traveled across Pennsylvania, down through Virginia and into North Carolina before returning home to New Jersey. Throughout their journey, they met, spoke to, visited and stayed with Quakers while observing the condition of slavery and appealing to slave owners to emancipate their slaves. Woolman wrote that whenever he dined or lodged with slave owners who lived at "ease on the hard labour of their slaves," he felt ill at ease and guilty, but when he resided with slave owners who worked alongside their slaves and treated them well, he felt better. Woolman recognized how slavery was destroying those societies in the South and the individual's faith in God. "I saw, in these southern provinces, so many vices and corruptions, increased by this trade and this way of life, that it appeared to me as a dark gloominess hanging over the land: and though now many willingly run into it, yet in future the consequences will be grievous to posterity!" Woolman wrote. He also traveled across New Jersey attending meetings, and in 1753, he published his writings on slavery.[9] Woolman's concern for mankind took him through New England, preaching against slavery and encouraging slave owners to at least teach their slaves to read and write.[10] Because of his influence, the Philadelphia Meeting voted in 1758 to urge its members to emancipate their slaves. This led to some Quakers freeing their slaves in the 1760s, with conditions. Quakers in both East and West New Jersey accepted these policies. Since many of these meetings were open, it's possible that slaves listened to these debates.[11] Emancipation as well as actual manumission would have been topics slaves and freedmen would have discussed together. Freedmen would have also encouraged slaves to seek their own emancipation.

According to Henry Cooley, the *Gazetteer of New Jersey* reported in 1745 that the colony had a total population of 61,383 people, 4,606 of them slaves. Most slaves lived in East Jersey, from around Sandy Hook north to Raritan Valley. The West Jersey counties of Burlington, Gloucester and Salem had the fewest slaves in the colony.[12] Those West Jersey counties were also Quaker-majority areas. However, as the colonies moved closer to breaking ties with Great Britain some things began changing for the worse for Blacks. The number of slaves in the colony increased to about 11,000 people, and slave codes remained severe—in fact, the most severe of all northern colonies'. Any White person could whip a slave found more than five miles from his master's residence without a pass, and because Whites viewed freed Blacks as lazy, a slave code included the requirement that masters pay their county twenty pounds each year for every slave freed. Also, freed Blacks were prohibited from owning land until 1776. Slave codes also had the effect of discouraging manumissions and limiting rights to free Blacks.[13] During the 1773–74 legislative sessions, Quakers petitioned the New Jersey legislature to remove the manumission bond for slave owners. The state assembly acted by amending the bill to allow slave owners to free slaves who were twenty-one years old but only if they could support themselves, pay taxes and meet the requirements for citizenship. Suffrage was not included in this, and Blacks could marry but not to Whites. The slave owner still had to post a bond for older slaves in order to free them, and all freed Blacks would continue to have restricted rights. The changes were fruitless. This bill did not get passed. It was tabled by East Jersey legislators who voted against it even though legislators from West Jersey were for it.[14]

Conflict from the American Revolution gave hope to both freed and enslaved Blacks that freedom and equality would be theirs also. But as historian Herbert Aptheker argued, many slaves would learn that the calls for freedom and fairness were meant to pertain only to Whites. Many Whites who fought were slave owners unwilling to emancipate their slaves, not even to have them join the Patriot army or militia.[15] Americans focused on liberty and rights, ideas Blacks already appreciated and desired. Yet those ideals exposed the contradiction between what White colonists said and how they treated Blacks, particularly slaves. This troubled some White New Jerseyans, especially the West Jersey Quakers who were the most vocal advocates for emancipation. But as pacifists, Quakers did not sanction war. This belief did not endear the Society of Friends to Americans seeking independence from Great Britain. Despite their belief, some Quakers still felt the need to speak out against the lack of concern for the enslaved. One of the most active voices was Burlington County Quaker Samuel Allinson, who wrote to the New Jersey Assembly urging it to stop slave importations and allow manumissions without a surety bond. Allinson worked hard to abolish slavery. Five months before Virginian Patrick Henry made his famous "give me liberty or give me death" speech, Allinson wrote to him addressing "the poor Negroes in Slavery. A case which never called louder for a candid consideration & just conclusions, than at a time when many or all the Inhabitants of N. America are groaning under unconstitutional impositions destructive of their Liberty."[16] In 1778, Allinson wrote to New Jersey governor William Livingston expressing his fear that America would not "prosper in a right manner" unless it freed its slaves. Livingston wrote him back, stating he held the same "sentiments" pertaining to slavery and had suggested manumission to the state assembly but the house did not think it was the right time to address this and asked him privately to withdraw his suggestion. Although he did, the governor promised to continue pushing for manumission, calling slavery "utterly inconsistent with the principles of Christianity and humanity."[17]

Two members of the wealthy and powerful Cooper family from Gloucester County also took up the antislavery mantel. Quakers David and John Cooper both saw slavery as opposing the natural rights of Blacks and criticized the institution. David anonymously wrote a pamphlet condemning slavery. In his 1783 condemnation, he recited the words of the Declaration of Independence and the Bible, then questioned Americans' complacency toward slavery, writing, "Who would believe the same persons whose feelings are so exquisitely sensible respecting themselves, could be so callous toward negroes, and the miseries which, by their arbitrary power, they wantonly inflict." He pointed out colonists' hypocrisy for asking God for deliverance from their oppressors while at the same time denying Blacks the benefit of their laws and freedom. To underscore his expression, Cooper then sent a copy of his pamphlet to George Washington, who acknowledged he read it by signing his copy.[18] David Cooper and Samuel Allinson practiced what they preached about emancipation. On December 22, 1774, the duo legally documented the manumission of five minor slave children born to a slave woman named Catherine, who died. The woman and children belonged to a Shrewsbury owner who died, and as part of his estate, the slaves were sold to another Shrewsbury man who intended to keep them as slaves. Allinson and Cooper persuaded the second owner to sell them the family. After Allinson and Cooper acquired them all, the mother died. Allinson and Cooper then established the children's manumission on reaching full age, when they could be freed. Until that time, the men made arrangements for the children's education.[19]

John Cooper was highly involved in revolutionary activities during the war. He served on county committees and was a member of the New Jersey Provincial Congress (1775–76), the Continental Congress (1776) and the committee that drafted the New Jersey constitution of 1776. In 1777, the New Jersey legislature met in the second-floor hall of the Indian King Tavern in Haddonfield for its sessions. There the legislators adopted the state's seal.[20] Although he was a Patriot, Cooper criticized slavery as immoral and antithetical to America's claim as a nation for freedom. In a September 20, 1780 petition printed in the *New Jersey Gazette*, he pled for the immediate abolition of slavery and admonished his fellow countrymen for pursuing their own liberty while ignoring real slaves among them and for disobeying the Bible. He wrote, "In our publick and most solemn declarations we say, we are resolved to die free;—that slavery is worse than death…and yet surprising as it may seem, we hold thousands of our fellow-men in slavery, and slumber on under the dreadful load of guilt—Worse than murders and yet at ease!"[21] Cooper also implored other members of the Society of Friends not to take on slaves and to release those they already had in bondage.[22] This was not just a suggestion on Cooper's part; he urged members of the Haddonfield and Woodbury meetinghouses to free their slaves or be disowned. By 1792, Quakers of the Haddonfield Meeting had freed all their slaves.[23]

Although Blacks fought in battles on both sides of the Revolutionary War, their presence was more complicated when it came to Patriots. Many Patriots were slave owners who wanted their enslaved neither freed nor involved in

Historic Indian King Tavern, Haddonfield. *Author's photo.*

the war. Others did not want the slaves freed but were willing to have them take their place in battle. This created a dilemma for Blacks: either join the British and fight for their own freedom or fight with Americans and remain slaves. Although Washington at first refused to accept Blacks as soldiers in the Continental army, he later relented.

As a result, some slaves fought for the Continental army in place of their owners and received their freedom afterward, while others, like Samuel Sutphen from New Jersey, were promised freedom for service but denied it after the war ended.[24]

Others fought for the British or Loyalist militias, taking them up on their offers of freedom for service. One Black man, a New Jersey slave named Titus, ran to British colonial governor Lord Dunmore in Virginia and joined his Ethiopian Regiment composed of Black slaves, then returned to New Jersey to terrorize Patriots as "Colonel Tye," a mighty and fierce warrior. As a guerrilla leader, Colonel Tye led a band of up to eight hundred Blacks, "mulattos" and Whites, successfully attacking Patriot fortifications and slaveholding estates, freeing slaves and indentured servants and capturing Patriot leaders, such as Monmouth County Militia leaders Barnes Smock and Joshua Huddy. After capturing Smock, Colonel Tye and his band took him to New York City and handed him over to the British. In another incident, Colonel Tye captured Huddy (who was born in Salem, New Jersey) in a bold nighttime attack at his home. In this incident, the marauders staged a gunfight outside the home while some band members attempted to enter. Huddy held off the band, firing muskets from windows as he ran from room to room. After subduing Huddy, Colonel Tye attempted to row his prey across a pond, intending to hand him over to the British or Loyalists. After Tye launched the boat from shore, Huddy managed to escape in dramatic form by jumping overboard as his Patriot friends fired on the boat. Colonel Tye was wounded and later died of an infection but not before making a name for himself among both the Americans and the British in the Battle of Monmouth. One must wonder: If the Americans, particularly White New Jersey slave owners, had freed their slaves to fight the British, would the war have been resolved earlier? At the end of the war, many Blacks who fought for the British evacuated with them to Canada, the Caribbean, Africa or Europe.[25] For some Blacks neither selection of fighting for the British or Patriots was right, so instead, they chose freedom through escape. Many wanted freedom so much that they were willing to flee their homes and families to be fugitives in far-off rural areas.

George Washington, commander-in-chief of the Continental army. *Courtesy of Library of Congress.*

The Revolutionary War produced a new nation dedicated to freedom, but seemingly only for White people. Some New Jersey Blacks found freedom waging war, either by joining the British and evacuating with them at the end of the conflict or by fleeing their homes and families to exist among Native American tribes; others took advantage of the turmoil to run away or hide out alone. A few slaves in the state were rewarded for their service with freedom by Americans, yet most New Jersey slaves remained in bondage during and after the Revolution. Despite their condition, the war for liberty was not a fruitless endeavor, for it inspired not only Whites but also slaves to desire what now seemed more tangible than ever before. The Quakers stimulated notions of freedom by first citing Christian biblical principles and then American values of liberty, both cherished ideals that were integral to how they viewed themselves and how Americans wanted their new nation to be represented to the world. All the while, Blacks were watching and listening. They internalized the rhetoric and discerned foes from allies in their freedom quest. Quaker agitation and the Revolution had uncorked the freedom genie, and New Jersey Blacks were ready to pursue their desire. Change was occurring in the state, particularly in South Jersey. The subtle shaking of salt from the salt-of-the-earth people was about to become a pour.

CHAPTER 2

"THE MYSTIC SPELL OF AMERICA"

Historian W.E.B. Du Bois argued, "The Mystic Spell of Africa is and ever was over all America." To him, Africans gave America some of "her sweetest songs…inspired her finest literature…[and] guided her hardest work."[26] But the greatest gift from slavery was the inspiration to heroism that was demonstrated in men and women dedicated to undoing the institution in America. This gift included the heralded actions of people on the national level—like John Brown, William Lloyd Garrison, Lydia Maria Child and Frederick Douglass, to name a few—and those of local people, such as John Rock, Abigail Goodwin, William Still and Harriet Tubman, who worked across South Jersey. These abolitionists all endeavored toward Black liberty. They essentially gave America's Declaration of Independence its *veritas*. South Jersey abolitionists in particular lived up to the John Brown quote, "Nothing so charms the American people as personal bravery."[27]

After the Revolutionary War ended, membership in the abolitionist movement in the state increased. In January 1793, the New Jersey Abolition Society was formed in Burlington; its mission was to end slavery. As a result, it supported gradual emancipation.[28] Seven years earlier, the state legislature passed an act to prevent the importation of slaves from outside the county or from any other state and to authorize manumission. This law made it illegal to bring slaves into the state and keep them there for over six months. It also allowed manumission by having slave owners execute a certificate signed by two overseers of the poor in their township and two justices of the peace in their county.[29] This was definitely a win for antislavery residents and slave

John Brown, abolitionist. *Courtesy of Library of Congress.*

owners, who previously had to post a bond to free slaves, who in turn had to meet other requirements.

FREE BLACKS AND SLAVES IN NEW JERSEY

Year	Total Population	Free Blacks	Slaves
1790	184,139	2,762	11,423
1800	211,949	4,402	12,422
1810	245,555	7,813	10,851
1820	277,575	12,460	7,557
1830	320,823	18,303	2,254
1840	373,306	21,044	674
1850	480,555	23,810	236

Source: U.S. Census, 1850 Comparison Table of Population.

The first U.S. Census taken after the Revolutionary War ended showed New Jersey had a free Black population of 2,762 and a slave population of 11,423. Yet by 1800, the U.S. Census showed the slave population had increased by 999 souls. In 1800, the majority of slaves were in North Jersey, while South Jersey had a little more than 500 slaves left. During the war, New Jersey slave owners were reluctant to emancipate their slaves, and by the end of the century, many Americans were losing interest in rights for all men. Abolitionists were discovering that people who previously supported their cause now had waning feelings toward freeing Blacks. According to Jeffrey M. Dorwart, in the lower townships of Cape May County, the number of slaves increased between 1774 and 1784 from 18 to 63. He argued that the increase occurred among the old whaler yeoman families, who may have failed to list the true number of slaves held, fearing high taxes on property. This county had the highest percentage of slaves out of all the West Jersey counties.[30] Interestingly, this county also had the smallest percentage of Quakers living there out of all South Jersey counties. The early settlers of Cape May County were English colonists involved in whaling. Many of them came from East Jersey, Connecticut and Long Island.[31]

Despite the change in some attitudes, abolitionists continued pressing, and in 1804, the state legislature passed an act for gradual emancipation.[32] The law made children born of slaves free after July 4, 1804, once they

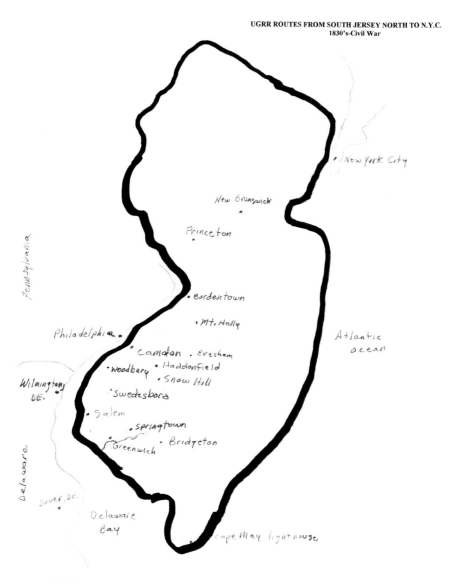

Map of UGRR routes, South Jersey to North Jersey. (Sources: Siebert, *Underground Railroad* and Wright, *Afro-Americans in New Jersey*.) *Author's drawing.*

reached age twenty-five, if male, and twenty-one, if female. It also provided slave owners with a way to make money from slave children by "abandoning" them to the state after caring for the child for one year. Owners were then compensated for this emancipation of the slave child, but the child was not free yet, just hired out to others until he or she reached the age of legal emancipation.[33]

Freedmen and Slaves

Slaves manumitted by Quakers in West Jersey during the 1700s became the freedmen of South Jersey in the 1800s. These freed Blacks began forming their own villages and communities across the region, such as Snow Hill, Springtown and Guineatown. These settlements were safe places for all Blacks—freed or fugitive—to live, worship and feel loved. Many of these Black communities began on land set aside for them by former Quaker slave owners or by Quaker businessmen. Examples are Springtown in Cumberland County, started by Blacks after 1810 on land Greenwich Quakers sold to them following the state's passage of the Manumission Act of 1786,[34] or the Camden City area known as Fettersville, built by Quaker businessman Richard Fetters. Fetters purchased land there in 1833, then divided it into lots for sale. Many Blacks from South Jersey and Philadelphia purchased those lots and constructed homes, stores and churches.[35] Guineatown, located above Timber Creek in Gloucester County, was started as a Black community after slave owners Joseph and William Hugg freed their slaves in 1812.[36] The Huggs were descendants of patriarch John Hugg, an Irish Quaker who settled in Gloucester County in 1683. His son, John Jr., became one of the county's largest slave owners; his slaves reportedly made up a large part of the Black population.[37] The settlement allegedly was so named because one of Hugg's emancipated slaves claimed to be from a royal family in Guinea, Africa.[38]

Those Black communities served not only as areas for Blacks to prosper but also as safe havens for fugitives. Residents found that in Black communities, they could obtain information on manumission legislation, abolitionist news and spiritual support. Mutual aid societies formed in those areas could provide welfare services, such as financial aid, charity and job placement.[39] Getting slaves to those safe havens was one of the responsibilities of the Underground Railroad (UGRR). New Jersey had three "important outlets" for the

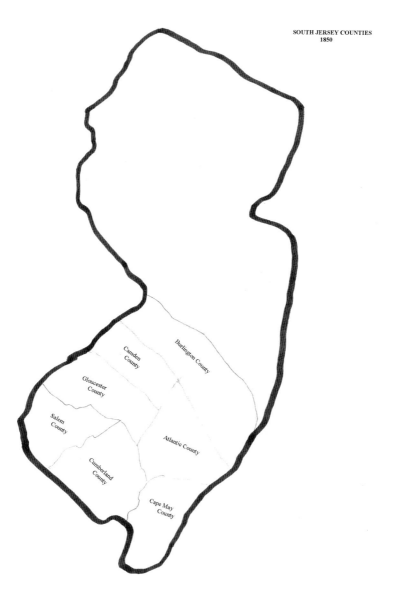

SOUTH JERSEY COUNTIES
1850

South Jersey counties, 1850 map. *Author's drawing.*

UGRR, according to Wilbur H. Siebert. The most important one ran from Philadelphia to Jersey City to New York City. Along this route, fugitives were moved from Philadelphia to Camden, through that county up to Burlington, then to Bordentown, Princeton, New Brunswick and Jersey City, where they were transported to Grand Central Station in New York City.

The second route ran across the Delaware River to the Salem area. It operated in cooperation with the Philadelphia route but acted independently the first sixty miles up to Bordentown. The first stage of this route ended at Woodbury, about twenty-five miles from Salem if the fugitive traveled on foot but about thirty-five miles if they were transported by wagon. The second stage ended at Evesham Mount before continuing from there to Bordentown.

The third route was the Greenwich Line in the swampy areas of Greenwich, Cumberland County, on the Delaware Bay, where free Blacks and Quakers lived. According to Siebert, fugitives were transported by boat at night from the Dover, Delaware region by crossing the Delaware Bay. Once they landed in New Jersey, fugitives were refreshed and taken to Swedesboro, then to Evesham Mount and on to Mount Holly, where they connected with the Philadelphia Line to go to New York.[40]

As a result, many if not all Black communities in South Jersey naturally became targeted spots for slave catchers. But they also became defensive centers, with people ready to repulse man stealers using overwhelming resistance and violence if necessary.

BROKEN SILENCE

The early January snow glistened in the cold night as the small family prepared to go to bed. The new year 1835 was just beginning, but it was full of hope for better days. As the family, which included a young mother and an infant, settled down, probably in one bed, the quietness of the night was suddenly and violently broken when the door to their cabin was forcibly burst open, awaking and startling the family. An armed White Philadelphia slave catcher named Donaho (sometimes spelled Donahue) rushed inside the cabin and stood over the Black family. He then forced all the barely dressed members out of their home, located a few miles outside Salem city. The violent commotion along with the sobbing, scared family forcibly rounded up like cattle and either compelled to walk the distance to Salem or huddled together in a wagon for the ride there probably stirred the sleeping community awake as to what was happening and excited emotions about this atrocious incident. Donaho brought the entire family to stand before Judge Ford at the Salem courthouse in hopes of having the suspected fugitives certified as runaways.[41]

Salem courthouse (where slave trials were held), Salem, New Jersey. *Author's photo.*

Under the Fugitive Slave Act of 1793, slave catchers were mandated to take suspected runaway slaves before a circuit, district or U.S. judge in that state to certify the arrest and get permission to remove the slaves. But slave catchers argued that because federal judges were on circuit, it was difficult to get cases before them in time and that taking prisoners before a local judge was risky because local residents could steal the fugitive. They also feared the judge could take his time deciding the case or refuse to side with the slave catcher.[42]

At the hearing, the courtroom was packed with Black people from the community who had heard about the arrest. Judge Ford reviewed the claim and found there were irregularities with the arrest and that not all the proper procedures were followed. The defense lawyer then spoke up, exclaiming, "Every word and letter of the law must be fulfilled before a human being can be taken from this community, and subjected to a life of endless slavery."[43] Judge Ford then dismissed the defendant, the slave woman, from the court after he "squashed" the warrant. The suspected slave mother cradled her baby in her arms after the ruling. She probably felt relieved this nightmare was over for her and thought she was safe. But before she could leave, the slave catcher, infuriated at the decision, refused to let it end with the judge's ruling. In an instant, Donaho jumped up and drew a pistol, pointing it at the young mother as he exclaimed he was going to protect his boss's slave property. The packed courtroom was filled with Black witnesses, many of whom were probably members of the same community, who had all heard about the arrest. Many may have even seen the violent incident occur during the night. The audience went wild at Donaho's action and quickly moved against him. At the same time, the courtroom constable grabbed Donaho's arm and took the pistol from him. Undaunted, Donaho pulled out a dagger, threatening the surging crowd. But a sheriff managed to disarm the slave catcher, probably as the crowd rushed him. During the scuffle and chaos, the young mother made her escape through a window with her baby. She was spirited off by some witnesses. Meanwhile, Donaho was immediately jailed for three to four days before the judge released him on bail. Unfortunately, the other members of the family were jailed for safekeeping while the matter was further investigated.[44]

The Black community of Snow Hill is located a few miles south of the historic colonial town of Haddonfield, founded by Quakers, which served as a meeting place for the New Jersey Provincial Congress during the Revolutionary War.[45] Snow Hill became one of the most important UGRR sites in South Jersey during the antebellum period because of Black residents' urgent desire to assist fugitives. In 1835, Snow Hill was a growing and safe settlement for Blacks to live, where the people worked hard and worshipped the Lord with all their hearts at weekly meetings in the woods. In August, the

Side view of
Salem courthouse.
Author's photo.

local Camden newspaper ran an advertisement about a "Colored People's Camp Meeting" to be held on the property of Joel G. Clark, located between Chew's Landing and Haddonfield. The camp meeting was scheduled to last for five days. Although the newspaper advertisement does not place the location in Snow Hill, it was close to the village. Many people reading the newspaper would have been alerted that this was a place where Black folk congregated.[46] So it should not have come as a surprise what happened two months later.

In October, the good people of Snow Hill were holding their weekly worship service in the woods when two strangers, Black men from Philadelphia, attended uninvited. Since Black worship services were usually open to all, it would not have caused a stir when new people arrived. After all, it was a common occurrence for fugitives to appear in Black communities looking for help or comfort. They would have been welcomed. Subsequent to the two strangers' arrival, another stranger presented himself at the service. The third man told congregants he, too, was from Philadelphia and had followed the other strangers there. He alleged that the other men were really spies sent to find out who was at the worship service and report back to slave catchers in the city. Once news of this revelation spread among the group—and it spread quickly—the worshippers grew angry and confronted the men. When the pair realized they were in harm's way, they attempted to flee. But worshippers were riled up at that point and caught the two intruders, then stripped and whipped them with three hundred lashes. Such a commotion was raised that White residents in the area heard it and responded to the agitation, attempting to rescue the men. As the local White people arrived, the Black worshippers all fled the area.[47]

The slave catcher Donaho (or Donahue) was an active and constant threat to fugitives and freedmen across South Jersey. As more and more slaves from the South ran north, slave catching became big business. Despite the heartless motivation—money—that these men and sometimes women had for dragging people back into bondage, another sinister reality was that often, freedmen were being captured and falsely claimed as fugitives. On January 6, 1836, a Woodbury, New Jersey newspaper reported an "outrage" concerning a slave-catching incident:

> We have just learned that a most gross outrage and riot occurred in Swedesboro in this county on Sunday night last. All the particulars we can gather are these, Donahue, a Constable from Philadelphia, a noted negro catcher, in company with some four or five others, apprehended on Saturday night a black man as being a slave, at Jarrett's Dam, and took him to Johnson's Tavern in Swedesboro, where he was kept in custody.[48]

The story did not end there. Once the Black community found out about the kidnapping, a group of people surrounded the tavern house. They came armed. Some carried guns; others held "brickbats and other missiles" to be used in rescuing the man. The account stated that the group broke all the windows, including the frames and sashes, in order to gain entry. All the while, gunfire erupted with both sides; the men shot "vollies" at each other all night until morning. Despite all-night shooting, only one person, an English peddler, was injured and not by the outsiders but by the men inside the house. The peddler apparently was at the tavern when the disturbance broke out. He hid in the garret and was shot in the knee by one of Donahue's men as he descended through a trapdoor. The shooters inside the house believed the peddler was one of the "besiegers" who had gained entry through the roof. The peddler was seriously injured and at risk of having his leg amputated. Although the standoff did not yield the prisoner, none of the assailants outside were caught by authorities.[49]

The following week, the prisoner was brought before Judge Ford on a writ of habeas corpus, but immediately, the judge saw irregularities. The writ by which the sheriff was holding the Black man purportedly was issued by court of common pleas judge Joseph B. Harker, but the document was missing the judge's seal. In addition, it appeared that another warrant on the same issue had been lodged against the prisoner and was dated the same day as the first warrant. The defendant's attorney, E.B. Caldwell, moved for dismissal of all charges based on the irregularities, but the claimant's lawyer argued for his client's rights to the Black man. The judge adjourned for a while, and the prisoner was re-jailed. His attorney then raised objections pointing to the nonconformity of actions and cited the state legislature's statute on the issue. This resulted in the judge releasing the man. Judge Ford then chided the officers that "strict compliance" was required in such cases.[50]

The Springtown community was often targeted by slave catchers, so residents were prepared when kidnappers arrived. Abolitionist Samuel Ringgold Ward lived near Springtown for several years as a child. He and his parents were fugitives who escaped to Greenwich on the UGRR and found work in the Cumberland County area. Ward wrote that his parents made a conscious decision to move to Cumberland County by obtaining the most accurate information on how and where best to escape. They learned that it was not necessary to run to Canada—just to New Jersey, where Quakers lived. Once they landed in Cumberland County in 1820, Ward wrote that they found many other Blacks living in Springtown and Bridgeton among Quakers such as the Bacons, Woods, Reeves and Lippincotts. Ward described these Quakers as true neighbors, "not loving in word and tongue" but in deed and truth. Whenever any slave catchers did come into the community, the Quakers chased them away by placing all kinds of "peaceful obstacles in their way, while the Negroes made it a little *too hot* for their comfort," Ward stated.[51]

An example of this kind of effort used to thwart both authorities and slave catchers was an incident in Bridgeton, just a few miles from Springtown. A Maryland slave catcher called on police to arrest a Springtown man on grounds he was a fugitive. The Black man was taken to the courthouse in Bridgeton for trial, but right before the trial started, the courtroom door was forced open by a group of Blacks, advised by a White abolitionist, who rushed in like a whirlwind, grabbed the suspected fugitive and dashed out

Early Greenwich Quaker meeting, Greenwich. *Author's photo.*

with him. The rescuers and the fugitive all escaped. As the officers of the law prepared to go look for them, they were told not to bother.[52] Newspaper reports did not disclose who told them not to pursue, but the sentiment may have been expressed by locals who knew better. The fugitive had absconded and would not be found.

Blacks were often thought to be slaves rather than freedmen, even though the state supreme court decided in *State v. Heddon* (1795) that White people needed to prove their ownership of any Black person they were trying to claim as a slave. But the Black person did not have to prove he was a free man, only that the White person did not have a right to claim him. The ruling asserted that just being held as property was not proof of claim.[53] Suspected fugitives should have been held to this ruling, yet apparently, this was not something runaways could rely on. So Black residents often took matters into their own hands and rescued those arrested, fearing they would not receive the benefit of the doubt.

Springtown residents took just as harsh a view toward Black informants as they did toward slave catchers. Sometimes, though, conflicts ended with tragic consequences. When one resident named Mews was accused of being an informant for a slave master who was arrested, the community decided to banish him. Mews went to work early, but on his way home, he was met by a party of women armed with clubs, axes and other weapons, ready to drive him away. Mews ran to his boardinghouse, owned by Levin Bond, but within minutes, it was surrounded by the women. Fearful of what was coming next, Bond demanded Mews leave. The tattler agreed to vacate the premises, but first, he wanted to pack his clothes. Mews, for some unknown reason, took too much time packing. Maybe he miscalculated the women's rage or thought he could wait them out. But another man named Chaney decided to intervene and force Mews out. Maybe Chaney sided with the women and wanted to get rid of someone who would betray his race. Or maybe, if he were an occupant of the boardinghouse, he feared the house would be damaged by the angry mob and decided to take matters into his own hands. Regardless, Chaney tried to force Mews out. As he did this, a scuffle ensued. Mews defended himself by using an axe against Chaney, inflicting a severe gash on Chaney's right breast and abdomen, mortally wounding the assailant. Mews did escape, but no account was given of how he made his way through the mob outside. The local newspaper blamed the Black residents and abolitionists for the deadly melee, criticizing their total disregard for the law.[54] Nothing was written about anyone being held responsible for the death.

Heaven Sent

Black churches in South Jersey played dual roles as institutions where the word of God was preached and the human condition was addressed. Ministers preached Bible verses such as Ephesians 4:5, exhorting believers to love and forgive one another, while reminding them to be strong like David when he fled before King Saul and was delivered from his enemy in Psalms 18. Congregants such as those in Macedonia AME Church in Camden showed they had no problem counterbalancing "And be ye kind one to another, tenderhearted, forgiving one another" (Ephesians 4:32) with "He teacheth my hands to war" (Psalms 18:34). Built in 1832, the church served the Black community spiritually, educationally, economically and socially. It was also thoroughly entrenched in the abolition movement due to its location and members.[55] According to church interpreter Ramona Cherey in an October 2013 interview, when the edifice was first constructed, it was about a block from the Delaware River. In the 1800s, there were several ferry landings in and near Camden, with the most popular landings being Cooper's Ferry at the foot of Cooper Street, and Kaighn's Ferry at Kaighn's Point, where ferries crossed over the Delaware River into Philadelphia.[56] All kinds of vessels, such as sailboats, steamboats, schooners and sloops, plied the waters of the Delaware River. Wharfs where vessels could dock lined both sides of the river, and many schooners and steamboats left landings in Camden for Cape May, making stops in New Castle in the slave state of Delaware. There, passengers could board or exit, and this city was also an exchange point for those heading south and wishing to catch the train to Baltimore or other southern points.[57] This access could be a very expedient way to transport fugitives back south via a slave state like Delaware.

Camden was a very familiar spot to slave catchers. For over one hundred years, Cooper's Ferry was a main arrival point for slaves brought to West Jersey and Philadelphia, with slave auctions held at the ferry landing.[58]

Since Camden was a major stop on the UGRR, slave catchers made it their business to traverse the town and county looking for prey. By 1847, Macedonia AME was the oldest, largest and most influential Black church in town. Its pastor was Reverend Thomas Clement Oliver, a UGRR conductor raised in a family active in the UGRR movement.[59] So the church was naturally ensconced in abolition. Like most Black churches of the era, Macedonia AME assisted fugitives in an unobtrusive manner, except for one day in 1847. Congregants were holding a prayer meeting at the house of worship when they heard an outcry coming from the street. Slave catchers had captured a man believed to be a fugitive and secured him in a wagon for transport to the ferry. As the wagon passed the church, the prisoner began yelling out, "Kidnappers!" The worshippers inside the church heard the cries and quickly ran out to see what was happening. They saw the Black man held captive and knew he would be irretrievably lost to bondage if that wagon reached the ferry landing. Without hesitation, the members surrounded the wagon, halting its progression. Then Hannah Bowen, a church member, reportedly cut the traces, freeing the horses from the wagon. The horses were then driven away, leaving stranded the men—fugitive and slave catchers—all surrounded by angry Black congregants and community members ready to act violently. A temporary standoff ensued, but the slave catchers knew they were on untenable ground. There was no way they could escape unscathed with the fugitive. As a result, they were forced to turn over the prisoner to the crowd in exchange for their own safe release.[60]

Southward view of the Delaware River from Camden. *Author's photo.*

Sign designating where slaves were sold at former Cooper's Ferry Landing spot, Camden. *Author's photo.*

Northeast view of Cooper Street (with historic buildings), Camden. *Author's photo.*

Not all abolitionists engaged in armed resistance. Many operated in a passive-aggressive mode or in a covert manner. Peter Mott, a free Black man, lived a very respectable life as a hardworking husband and resident of Snow Hill. During the day, he worked hard as a farmer, laborer and plasterer, plying his trade in neighboring towns like Camden and Haddonfield.[61] On Sundays, Mott served as Sunday school superintendent at his local church, Mount Pisgah African Methodist.[62] An industrious man, Mott was a major landowner in Snow Hill.[63] And he owned his own home, built in 1845—a major accomplishment for a Black man in antebellum New Jersey. The white clapboard two-story home with a basement stood as a testament to what hardworking freedmen could achieve.[64] Mott truly was a cornerstone of his community. However, there was another side to him. At night, he was a hardworking, diligent operator and stationmaster on the "Lightning Train," another name for the Underground Railroad.[65] Under the cover of darkness, he opened his home to fugitives. Mott worked with Philadelphia abolitionists such as William Still, a leading UGRR conductor and worker with the Pennsylvania Anti-Slavery Society, to move runaway slaves north.[66]

As Mott was a farmer, laborer and plasterer known around the area, it would not have been out of place to see him traveling across the

Above: Historic Macedonia AME Church, Camden. *Author's photo.*

Right: Closeup of stained glass windows, historic Macedonia AME Church. *Author's photo.*

Left: Peter Mott House, Lawnside. *Author's photo.*

Below: Side view of shed at Peter Mott house. *Author's photo.*

William Still, abolitionist and UGRR conductor. *Courtesy of Library of Congress.*

county in a wagon full of crates or barrels, seemingly filled with supplies or produce. But as a clandestine operator, he could easily transport fugitives from one UGRR station in Camden to another in Haddonfield with no one the wiser. Mott's UGRR activity needed to remain covert to protect not only the slaves but also himself. If it was revealed, his family and home could have been put in jeopardy by slave catchers, his effectiveness as a conductor would have ended and livelihood might have been ruined.

At his death, William Still was called the "Father of the Underground Railroad" by the *New York Times.* In 1847, Still started working with the Pennsylvania Anti-Slavery Society as a clerk and janitor. He quickly proved his worth helping fugitives on the UGRR. He became a conductor in 1850 when he was appointed chairman of the Acting Vigilance Committee formed in response to the Fugitive Slave Law enacted that year. In this capacity, Still alerted slaves brought to Pennsylvania of the law freeing them, like in the case of Jane Johnson or that of Robert Thompson from Hightstown, New Jersey, who fled from his cruel master who threatened to kill him.[67] Still was responsible for transporting many other runaway slaves to safety, and his desire for this work came naturally. The Burlington County native was born to slave parents. His father, Levin, purchased his freedom and moved to New Jersey. His mother, Charity, was a fugitive slave who fled to the state to be with her husband. Her journey was not a smooth one. She had two flights to freedom, the first ending after she was caught with her four children by slave catchers and returned to her owner. Soon after her retrieval, she escaped again but with only her two young daughters. She made the heartbreaking decision to leave her two sons in slavery, believing she could not successfully escape with all four children. On reaching New Jersey, she found her husband, and they moved to the woods of Burlington County and continued raising their family. Still grew up hearing those harrowing stories of escape and freedom and how his two older brothers were left behind. His family's history developed a passion in him to help liberate others in bondage.[68] Still was involved in assisting hundreds of

Historic Stimson-Woolston House, Cooper Street, Camden (example of high style pre–Civil War architecture). *Author's photo.*

runaways to freedom in the North and Canada. He had a profound effect on the lives of people fleeing slavery and was an instrumental aid to UGRR operators and stationmasters in the region. His book, *The Underground Railroad*, was a record of clandestine escapes and outright confrontations with slave owners who took their slaves to Philadelphia, where they were legally free. It is a testament to his courage, tenacity and love of freedom.

Two extraordinary stationmasters were Quaker sisters Abigail and Elizabeth Goodwin from Salem. The pair operated a UGRR station from their Market Street home, hiding fugitives until they could be forwarded to the next station. To further assist escaped slaves, the Goodwin sisters headed donation drives to collect food, clothing and medicine from the community. The sisters also used their home as a center for local abolitionists.[69]

William Still respected both women for their UGRR work, but he especially esteemed Abigail for her unwavering commitment. He wrote in his record of the UGRR that "Betsy economized greatly in order to give to the cause, but Abby denied herself even *necessary apparel*….Giving to the colored people was a perfect *passion* with her; consequently she was known

Colonial-era buildings across the street from Indian King Tavern (on Haddon Avenue), Haddonfield. *Author's photo.*

Abigail Goodwin house, Salem. *Author's photo.*

Goodwin house, side yard garden view. *Author's photo.*

as a larger giver than Betsy." Not only did Abigail deprive herself of decent clothing, but she was also a better writer than Betsy and communicated with other abolitionists. "She worked for the slave as a mother would work for her children," Still remarked.[70]

One of the abolitionists Abigail hosted was famed captain of the *Pearl* Daniel Drayton, after he was released from jail in 1852 as a result of abolitionists' pressure on President Millard Fillmore.[71] Drayton, an abolitionist from Cumberland County, New Jersey, worked as a ship captain.[72] In 1847, Drayton was asked to rescue a mother and five children from slavery in Washington, D.C. The mother was about to be sold away from her children even after the owner had been paid to set her free. Drayton agreed and ended up transporting the mother, her children and another female relative to freedom. This successful clandestine trip presented another opportunity for the captain to help more slaves escape bondage. On April 15, 1848, the captain attempted to secretly transport seventy-six slaves from Washington, D.C., to freedom in the North.[73] The *Pearl* only made it as far as the confluence of the Potomac River and the Chesapeake Bay before being captured by a posse less than twenty-four hours later.[74] Although Drayton failed in rescuing those slaves, his action brought attention to slavery in

Colonel Robert Gibbon Johnson house, Salem, where abolitionist and runaway Amy Hester Reckless was enslaved. *Author's photo.*

the nation's capital, resulting in Congress banning the slave trade in the District of Columbia under the Compromise of 1850.[75] The compromise was promoted by Kentucky representative and slave owner Henry Clay, who believed Congress had the right to legislate slavery in D.C. even though he supported slavery in the states.[76]

Another abolitionist who worked closely with Abigail Goodwin was Amy Hester (Hetty) Reckless. Reckless was born into slavery in Salem in 1776 and later freed herself. Her mother, Dorcas Boadley, was owned by the mother of Colonel Robert Gibbon Johnson, so Reckless grew up in the Johnson household and moved along with them to the new home on Market Street built in 1806 by the colonel. Taking her freedom into her own hands, Reckless decided to flee enslavement with her children after the colonel's second wife harshly mistreated her.[77] She found freedom in Philadelphia, where she resolved to help others by joining the UGRR. Reckless settled into a home, then opened it to fugitives as a UGRR station. Pennsylvania conductor James T. Dannaker often relied on Reckless to hide fugitives when other stations were full. As a cautious conductor, Dannaker always had several places to call on in case of danger. He instituted a specific way of announcing himself at stations, reportedly by "three distinct raps on the door." The stationmasters understood the raps and had been warned to take precautions before opening the door, especially if they had other people inside. On one trip, Dannaker tried to find lodging for a group of eight fugitives who arrived together from Norfolk, Virginia. He could not find any homes available until he reached the Reckless house. Reckless took them all in, including Dannaker, who had business in the city the next day.[78] This was usual for the senior citizen, who well understood the feelings and needs of fleeing slaves since she herself had been one. Her generosity, compassion and fearlessness were typical traits of Salem Blacks, evidenced by Dannaker's belief that he could always rely on her. Reckless tirelessly worked alongside Lucretia Mott in the Philadelphia Anti-Slavery Society and was active in the anti-prostitution movement and a supporter of Black Sabbath schools.[79]

Plot and Reap

Fugitives fleeing to Greenwich could find refuge in several places. One place was the Sheppard gristmill, which served area farmers who needed grain ground into flour or meal and as a community meeting place. The mill was started by Quaker John Sheppard, who left it and a forested tract to his son Benjamin, who continued operating the mill. As fugitives came into the area, Benjamin took on the additional role of operator on the UGRR, feeding and providing safe hiding places for them in the woods and bogs surrounding his mill. Benjamin also offered fugitives a chance to earn an acre of his land on which to live by working for him.[80]

The Black church Bethel Othello AME in Springtown serviced residents in this stronghold community and stood as a bold UGRR stop, providing reassurance to fugitives crossing the Delaware Bay. UGRR operators Julia and Algy Stanford lived next door to the church and actively participated in helping runaways by manning oars on boats that cast off from shore and rowed out to meet boats bringing "flying bondsmen." According to church interpreters Naomi and Julia Morris, the Stanfords also kept an eye out for slave catchers who frequented the community and church looking for runaways and would ring the church's bell, sounding the alarm, whenever slave catchers were sighted in the area.[81]

The Morris sisters also explained that Bethel Othello AME was often visited by Harriet Tubman, who brought fugitives there for sustenance and shelter before heading off to the next station.[82] If Tubman traveled overland, she would have had to cross several waterways, such as Stow Creek, Lower Alloways Creek or marshland along the lower regions of Salem and Cumberland Counties in the Mad Horse Creek State Wildlife Management Area in order to reach Springtown or Greenwich. If fugitives were brought across the bay, there were many safe sites on which to land, including a fishing village at the mouth of Stow Creek and the Delaware Bay called Cavier Point near Greenwich, where runaways could safely disembark from boats. This site was remote, and the docks were manned by Black oyster workers. Other landings were also possible along Stow Creek as it flowed into the interior of Cumberland County. Lisa Garrison, a Greenwich tour

Historic Bethel Othello AME Church, Springtown. *Courtesy of the Vineland Historical and Antiquarian Society.*

Mad Horse Creek and marsh looking southward toward Delaware Bay. *Author's photo.*

Forested area of Mad Horse Creek, Salem County. *Author's photo.*

interpreter, stated that abolitionists bringing fugitives across the bay had a special signal—flashing blue and yellow lights in sequence—to signal comrades on shore that a boat needed to meet them to pick up cargo.[83] This information is confirmed by historian Wilbur H. Siebert, who wrote this about the Greenwich Line: "Slaves were transported at night across the Delaware River from the vicinity of Dover, in boats marked by a yellow light hung below a blue one, and were met some distance out from the Jersey shore by boats showing the same lights."[84] Siebert contended that abolitionists liked using waterways to transport fugitives and that Thomas Garrett was known to send them by steamboat from Wilmington, Delaware, to Philadelphia.[85]

Black watermen had a secret communication network to help fugitives escaping from coastal areas. They knew where Quakers and other sympathetic Whites lived, and they knew of safe places for runaways to come ashore. Tubman learned of this secret communication network from Black watermen when she worked alongside them as a slave in Maryland. Around the mid-1840s, Tubman was permitted to hire herself out to other Whites in the area. She began doing hard labor driving oxen, carting

Mad Horse Creek and marsh looking southward toward Delaware Bay as it meets the horizon, Salem County. *Author's photo.*

Stow Creek (southward view). *Author's photo.*

Wooded area bordering Stow Creek, Cumberland County side, looking southeast. *Author's photo.*

Meadow on Salem County side of Stow Creek, looking northwest. *Author's photo.*

materials and plowing alongside men doing the same jobs. She was such a good worker that she was able to earn enough money to purchase a pair of steers. She was also able to work for her father, Benjamin Ross, a freedman who had jobs inspecting and supervising the cutting and hauling of timber to the docks on the Chesapeake Bay for shipment to Baltimore.[86] Ross was employed by his former owner Dr. Anthony Thompson, who purchased about 2,100 acres of forested land in Poplar Neck, Maryland, on the Choptank River. Tubman also worked at another site in Madison owned by the Stewart family. At this site, located on the Chesapeake Bay below Cambridge, she came into contact with the Black watermen who informed her of the secret communication network.[87] It is possible that the flashing of colored lights used by boatmen in the Delaware Bay was part of that secret Black code. Black watermen worked on docks and ships, at ports and harbors, and came into contact with other Black seamen who traveled across the Eastern Seaboard to ports. These men were the hubs of the communication wheel spreading news, gossip and information, and they secreted messages and letters between freedmen and the enslaved.[88]

The Cooper River served as an important waterway facilitating trade and commerce to the Camden County area. It flowed from the interior of the county out to the Delaware River crossing through the populated areas of Haddonfield and Camden and subsequently played a role in abolition. The Croft Farm, located off the river, served as a notable UGRR station. Known as Edgewater at Evans Pond, it was named by owner Josiah "Cy" Bispham Evans, who assisted fugitives coming from Camden and heading north. The property dates to the late 1600s and was the site of gristmills from 1697 to 1897.[89] In 1816, Joel and Thomas Evans purchased the property and continued milling operations. Thomas also began assisting fugitives on the UGRR, providing shelter and food. In 1844, Thomas's son, Josiah, became owner, named it Edgewater and continued UGRR activities. Both Josiah and his father were members of the Abolition Society, and Josiah's grandfather Enoch was a member of the New Jersey Society for Promoting Abolition. In 1918, Josiah's grandson Walter Evans wrote about his family's UGRR activities, stating that runaways were brought over from as far as Woodbury and hidden inside the house's attic or outside in haystacks. They were fed and then, in the middle of the night, concealed in a covered wagon and taken to the next station in Mount Holly.[90]

One fugitive that Thomas Evans helped was Joshua Saddler, a fugitive from Maryland who fled in the 1830s. Once he arrived at Edgewater, he was allowed to stay on and work on the farm. Saddler was able to save enough money to purchase his own property, a 25.8-acre old-growth forested lot a short distance from the Croft Farm. He built a home there and then offered his woods as a haven for other fugitives. Later known as Saddlertown, this site gave sanctuary to many escaped slaves. Today, the forested lot is called Saddler's Woods and stands preserved as a testament to the charity of both Saddler and Evans.[91]

The town of Swedesboro in Gloucester County was on the UGRR route, and one site played a significant dual role in the town's early Swedish history as well as its abolition history. The town was part of a larger Swedish settlement established along the Delaware River from Mantua Creek down to Raccoon Creek in 1638. The Swedish settlers built early log cabin homes out of timber in the area using the dovetail locking method and no nails. Cracks between the logs were filled in with a mixture of straw or grass and clay forming a paste, which hardened during the winter and could be chipped away in the summer for ventilation.[92] One original log cabin constructed on the Morton Mortenson Grand Sprute Plantation, a Swedish farm located along Raccoon Creek, was built either as a first shelter for the

Above: Historic Trinity Swedish Church, Swedesboro. *Author's photo*.

Left: Historic Mount Zion AME Church, Swedesboro. *Author's photo*.

property owner or as a crib for animals. During the 1800s, it was also used as a way station for fugitives on the UGRR. Reportedly, runaways coming up from Salem or those dropped off along Raccoon Creek utilized the log cabin, staying overnight or for a few hours before continuing on to Mount Zion AME Church, situated about two miles north of Swedesboro. In 1989, the log cabin was moved from its former location along the creek to behind the historic Swedish Trinity Church in Swedesboro.

Mount Zion AME Church was founded in 1799 on land Quakers put aside for emancipated slaves. The one-story frame church was originally built in 1834 and played an important role on the UGRR; congregants provided fugitives with food, supplies, shelter and protection. Inside the vestibule was a secret trapdoor on the floor, giving access to a crawlspace used to hide runaways. After being refreshed, fugitives were transported to the next station in Woodbury.[93]

Abolitionists, both Black and White, living in South Jersey openly defied the slave law and battled slave catchers determined to return people seeking freedom to enslavement. They were willing and able to fight back using impediments both turbulent and temperate to achieve their goal of liberty for fugitives. These salt-of-the-earth people were determined to be not "good for nothing or cast out and trodden underfoot," as the Lord warned in Matthew 5:13–14, but a light to the world. Yet more needed to be done, and others were prepared to step up.

CHAPTER 3

CAPE MAY BY THE SEA

SUN, SAND AND ESPIONAGE

Cape May is a seaside town located at the southernmost end of the state, tagged "America's Oldest Seashore Resort" by town officials.[94] Originally known as Cape Island, it is separated from the mainland by the Cape May Canal and Cape May Harbor and fronts the Atlantic Ocean and Delaware Bay. The county's position makes New Jersey the only northern state to have part of its territory fall below the Mason-Dixon Line on a longitude closer to Arlington, Virginia.[95] The longitude and latitude coordinates of Cape May Point are: longitude -74.965385, latitude -38.937168. The coordinates for Arlington are: longitude -77.1067698, latitude -38.8799697.[96]

Yeomen and Slaves

Native Americans from the Lenni Lenape nation, members of the Kechameche tribe were the original inhabitants of the land. The first White settlers were English colonists from Connecticut and Long Island who pursued the whaling industry.[97] Their first settlement called Portsmouth or Town Bank was located on a bank on the Cape's Bay side and consisted of a few temporary buildings. It is believed these whalers arrived around 1635 and conducted whaling throughout the eighteenth century, although whaling here was most lucrative before 1775.[98]

The first African slaves were introduced on the cape in 1688. It is believed slaves and Indigenous people were involved in shore whaling along with Whites there.[99] Both Africans and Indigenous people were also enslaved by White settlers in New Jersey, and as a result, many intermarried.[100] Since whaling on the cape lasted only a few months during the year, White whalers and slaves found other work during the offseason. These White whalers began buying land for homesteads and cultivation and became whaler/ yeomen and freeholders, giving them the right to vote. Other White residents started businesses in logging, operating sawmills cutting cedar shingles and herding cattle on the barrier islands.[101] As the business and agricultural activity increased, so did the slave population, from five slaves in 1688 to over fifty in 1750, more than 90 percent of them owned by the original whaler/yeomen families. Male slaves sometimes worked alongside their owners, doing manual labor digging wells or ditches, farming, shipbuilding, working in mills and mining cedar timber from swamps. Slaves were also heavily utilized in all areas of the maritime industry as seamen, rope and sail makers, shipbuilders and dockworkers.[102]

Female slaves also performed fieldwork and farm work, digging ditches and clearing land, as well as domestic work, such as cooking, laundry, cleaning, sewing, childcare/nursing, weaving, candle-making and preserving food. Being pregnant did not exempt them from work. Since these yeomen households and farms were smaller than plantations, most textile production was performed at home by mistresses and slaves.[103]

Getting to the cape during the colonial period took patience and time. The easiest way was to take a boat or ship down the Delaware River or along the coast. Overland was another matter. Paths or Indian trails ran on dry land from the point up through the county to the Great Egg Harbor, but the terrain in the western part of the county made it a lot more difficult to cross over into the peninsula since it contained the Great Cedar Swamp, composed of old-growth pine, oak and cedar forests.[104] Coming from the coastline, travelers would find that a marsh extended from the shore inland for three miles. Residents built the first road from Cold Springs near the Point up to Egg Harbor in 1706.[105] Because this road flooded constantly, the colony assembly passed an act requiring a new road be built from present-day Mt. Pleasant up to Tuckahoe, crossing over the Great Cedar Swamp into what was then Salem County (now Cumberland County). In the mid-1700s, stagecoaches began running to Cape May with stops in towns along the way.[106] A stage from Philadelphia traveled to Woodbury, Glassboro, Malaga, Port Elizabeth and Dennisville to Cape May and the point. This route totaled about eighty-four miles, with the stage traveling between seven and nine miles per hour.[107] It could take up to twenty hours to travel from Camden to Cape May, with the stage leaving at about four o'clock in the morning and arriving around midnight.[108] The term *stagecoach* came about because travel was done in stages, with stops at inns or taverns for meals, drinks, personal relief and to change horses.[109]

By 1800, slavery had run its course in Cape May County. Beginning in 1802, slave owners, many of them whaler/yeomen, started manumitting their slaves. Jeffrey M. Dorwart reported a total of forty-three slaves freed between 1802 and 1834 in the county.[110] At the same time these masters were relinquishing their chattel, they began investing in more businesses and construction projects. Dorwart argued this was possibly done with an eye toward making the shore area a resort. Yet as Blacks were freed, they were released from bondage with no resources, property or place to go.[111] As a result, these newly freed men settled in dense forests and began communities. One of the oldest Black communities in the county, located on an old Indian trail (near the present-day airport) in Erma, was started by four people:

Cape May Point map, 1850s. (Source: Dorwart, *Cape May County*.) *Author's drawing*.

Lewis Cox, brothers Edward and Henry Turner and Mrs. Josephine Gibbs, who purchased land and then built homes.[112]

In spring 1821, Cape May County opened an almshouse two miles north of Cape May Courthouse in the center of the county. Officials touted that its purpose was to maintain order and provide for the poor. White residents contributed food and supplies, and its first occupants were mentally ill, sickly White residents and pregnant women (probably unwed), all family members of the county's gentry. Black people were left out until a lawyer advised two residents of their legal responsibilities to take care of former slaves who were too old or unable to work. Later that year, the almshouse began taking in Blacks who qualified. Thereafter, former slaves made up the majority of its residents until 1850, because slave owners manumitted their chattel who were too young, too old or too sick to work or care for themselves.[113]

As the century progressed, more and more Black communities began to be established around the county near Swainton, Goshen and on the cape. Siggtown was developed between a Black church (most likely Macedonia Baptist) and the Seashore Road on the island by members of the Seagrave, Armour and Wright families.[114]

Latitude: Resort

Cape May began its upswing toward becoming a major resort in 1815 with a sloop providing regular service between the island and Philadelphia. The next year, the *Delaware*, a wood-burning sidewheel steamboat, began operating from Philadelphia to New Castle, Delaware, where passengers from Baltimore, Washington, D.C., and other southern locations could board a sloop for the cape. Schooners also made trips between Philadelphia and Cape May. In 1819, the first regular steamboat service from the city to the cape without a transfer to a sloop commenced, with the steamboat *Vesta* departing from a wharf above Market Street in Philadelphia at two o'clock in the afternoon every Monday and Tuesday, stopping at Chester, Pennsylvania; New Castle; and Port Penn, Delaware, to pick up passengers before reaching the cape. At the island terminal, the steamboat would dock for only a few hours before heading back to the city.[115] By 1827, many steamboats were taking on southern passengers headed for the resort. Because of the increased boat traffic, officials realized they needed to establish an efficient way to transport baggage and people to the various hotels. During peak season in

Cape May Point. *Author's photo.*

the most prosperous years, up to three hundred carriages, omnibuses and wagons reportedly awaited the arrival of passengers at the terminal on the Point, eager to take them to their destinations.[116]

Getting to Cape May from the South was an adventure in itself. Southerners boarded a steamboat at Baltimore for Frenchtown, Maryland, located on the Elk River, where they would transfer to a stagecoach headed to New Castle, Delaware. At New Castle, passengers boarded the steamboat that departed from Philadelphia set for Cape May. In 1832, the New Castle and Frenchtown Railroad was constructed between those two towns so that passengers could get to the cape faster. This new train line ran from fifteen up to thirty miles per hour and left New Castle every morning at eight thirty; it returned leaving Frenchtown at ten thirty in the morning. Another train departed New Castle for Frenchtown every evening, except Sundays, around six o'clock and returned around nine o'clock. The fare was fifty cents. Robert Crozer Alexander noted, "On July 27th [1833] passengers on the Citizens' Union Line from Philadelphia to Baltimore were conveyed from New Castle to Frenchtown by the locomotive engine, a distance of sixteen miles and a quarter, in one hour and thirteen minutes. Henceforth, travelers from Baltimore and the South would be conveyed on the overland part of their journey by the railroad."[117]

As more and more steamboat operators competed for the Cape May trade, people other than southerners began coming to the island. Large steamboats also ran from New York bringing northerners to the resort. The trip from Gotham to Cape May took twelve hours.[118] A story reprinted in the *Cape May Star and Wave* newspaper in 1954 recounted one traveler's experience on a steamer from Baltimore to Cape May in 1900. The traveler, W.C. Steuart, stated his trip began at seven o'clock in the morning from Pier 10, Light Street, where he boarded the two-hundred-foot paddlewheel steamer *Queen Anne*. The steamer passed Fort McHenry and shoved up the Chesapeake Bay to Queenstown, Maryland, where he disembarked and then boarded a train for Lewes, Delaware. From there, he took another steamboat for Cape May. The entire trip took about five hours.[119] Although this route was a little different than earlier routes to the cape in the 1850s, Steuart's account speaks to the excitement of travel on the water on trips to the shore resort. "The present generation," he wrote, "knows nothing of the peace, serenity, and comfort of traveling aboard [steamers], up the picturesque rivers of the Eastern Shore."[120]

The first rooming house in Cape May was built in 1800 and could hold ten to twelve visitors.[121] By 1828, there were about twenty houses providing

Congress Hall, Cape May. *Author's photo.*

rooming services. The largest was built by Thomas Hughes, a descendant of one of the original whaler/yeomen families. Hughes's hostelry was three stories high, with a large ground-floor dining room and partitioned rooms for lodging on the other floors. It could hold about one hundred people, and the cost for room and board for a week was ten dollars. Many of Hughes's neighbors called this large building Tommy's Folly, but Hughes called it the Large House or Big House. In 1828, he had it ceremoniously christened Congress Hall. His intention was to attract prosperous and prominent families from Philadelphia, Delaware, Baltimore and Virginia, according to George F. Boyer.[122] Congress Hall was a large frame building, 108-feet long, constructed on the corner of Perry Street and Washington Avenue. Guests were fed fresh seafood, local game and meat brought in from Philadelphia.[123]

Over the next twenty-five years, Cape May would grow into a major resort town with construction of accommodations from cottage hotels that housed about a dozen visitors to enormous three- to four-story buildings that could hold thousands of guests. Hotels there began to be constructed with decorative embellishments, modern conveniences and offered amenities. The Mansion House, built in 1832 on four acres of land, was the first on the cape to have machine-cut wood trim and plastered walls. The Mount

Vernon Hotel was another large hostelry, with 482 rooms and a dining room that could seat 3,000 people when it opened in 1853.[124] By 1855, the hotel was undergoing construction to expand the facility from one built for up to 2,100 people to one that could hold a maximum of 3,500 guests. It was four stories tall, one floor higher than Congress Hall, and 300 feet long, with two wings, each 506 feet long. It was lit by gas piped throughout the building, and the dining room, which was 425 feet long, had over forty gas-burning chandeliers. It could seat more than 750 people at one time. The hotel touted a barber shop for men's personal grooming, pistol galleries and ten-pin bowling alleys for male guests. The ladies could enjoy the archery tent, an arena for horse shows or races and a quoits-pitching section. A stable and carriage house was also available.[125]

Other hotels also offered similar amenities and different ones, such as billiards, horseback riding on the beach and dances. These dances, or hops, were popular events for the tourists. The best bands from Philadelphia and New York—nationally known famous ensembles—were brought in to entertain and serenade guests.[126] The highlights of the season were the grand gala balls held in the immense dining rooms at the largest hotels. At these events, elites from the North and South would dance all night or sit on the verandahs of the large hotels in the moonlight. During the day, guests could bathe in the sea, walk the promenade or frequent gambling clubs.[127] The most popular gambling spot was the Blue Pig, a two-story frame house located near Congress Hall, owned by gambler Harry Cleveland.[128] Congress Hall was not to be outdone by the other hotels. Every afternoon at about four o'clock, the men gathered on the hotel's expansive lawn for a game called town ball, consisting of up to thirty men who played ball until seven o'clock.[129]

Southern planters, Dixie legislators and southern belles flocked to the cape in the summer. Cape May became a vacation destination and playground for them because the South had no shore resorts of its own before the Civil War. Coming to the cape for the summer was their way of escaping the southern summer heat and letting loose.[130] In 1834, an estimated seven hundred visitors, both northerners and southerners, were on the cape at all times during the summer. By 1849, large steamboats were carrying two hundred people at a time there. Some wealthy guests even brought their own grandiose carriages with showy teams of thoroughbred horses attended by their private Black coachmen.[131] By 1850, it was estimated seventeen thousand visitors had traveled to the cape, according to Wilson. In 1860, southerners spent over $50,000 at the resort.[132]

CAPE MAY ISLAND HOTELS 1828–58

American	Merchant's Hotel
Cape Island House	Mount Vernon
Central Hotel	National Hall
Centre House	New Atlantic
City Hotel	New Jersey House
Columbia Hotel	Ocean House
Commercial Hotel	Philadelphia House
Congress Hall	Tremont House
Delaware House	Tontine Hotel
Franklin House	Union House
Hughes Hall	U.S. Hotel
Irving House	Washington Hotel
Lafayette House	White Hall
Mansion House	

Sources: McMahon, Historic South Jersey Towns, *and Salvini,* Summer City.

CAPE MAY ISLAND HOTELS ACCOMMODATION MAXIMUMS, 1856

Mount Vernon	2,100 people
Columbia House	600
Congress Hall	500
Mansion House	300
Atlantic Hotel	300
U.S. Hotel	300
Ocean House	250
Centre House	200
National Hall	200
Delaware House	150

Hotels with 125 Persons Maximum

American Hotel	Tremont House
City Hotel	Washington House

Hotels with 100 Persons Maximum

Cape Island House	Merchant's Hotel
Commercial Hotel	Philadelphia House
Franklin House	Tontine Hotel
Irving House	Union House
Lafayette House	White Hall

Source: Alexander, Ho! For Cape Island.

Fun was the name of the game for elites who traveled to Cape May, and it was the place to be seen. Everyone from politicos to presidents came to the resort town. U.S. president James Buchanan visited in 1835, staying at Congress Hall, and Franklin Pierce came in 1855 and was given a reception by the town. Henry Clay, the great orator and backer of compromise, caused a sensation when he visited in the 1840s. Clay began coming to Cape May after his son died in the Mexican War (1846–48), and in 1847, Clay stayed at the Mansion House.[133] Historian H.W. Brands argued that Clay's talent was his ability to find a compromise that all sides could accept and this endeared him to White Americans. Clay thought up the Missouri Compromise, which allowed Maine to come into the Union as a free state and Missouri as a slave state. In 1850, he touted a compromise that admitted California as a free state, established New Mexico as a free territory, transferred Texas's debt to the United States, abolished the slave trade in Washington, D.C., but did not end slavery there, made fugitive slave laws more effective and took away Congressional power over the slave trade, leaving it up to the slave states.[134] Both compromises averted secession by the southern states. Guests visiting the cape looked for distinguished or notable figures such as Clay. There were also many who traveled to the cape just to attract the attention of the opposite sex. Many southern men assumed titles they did not earn, such as general, colonel or judge, to impress the ladies. Author Robert Crozer Alexander contended that one visitor to the cape divided the crowd of northerners and southerners into two camps: "In our definition of society here, we shall simply divide it into two parts, the Baltimorians and the Philadelphians, premising, however, that it requires a delicate touch to separate them they are so intimately interwoven."[135] In particular, Alexander argued, women in these two camps were judged for their beauty.

South Jersey resident Isaac Mickle also visited Cape May in 1843. Mickle, descended from an early immigrant to West Jersey who arrived in the late

Isaac Mickle, Camden County resident and diarist. *Courtesy of Gloucester County Historical Society.*

1600s as part of the Quaker migration, grew up in a wealthy family and was well educated, talented, a socialite and a staunch Democrat. He kept a diary for eight years recording local and national events and politics.[136] His trip to Cape May speaks to how visitors people-watched and socialized. He wrote:

> *18 July, Tuesday. Cape May.*
>
> *This morning my aunt Rachel, cousin Emma and I started for the Capes in the Steam-boat* Trenton, *which the Rail Road Company are running in opposition to Wildin's boat. We left Walnut Street wharf at nine o'clock and reached the landing at the Cape about five, after a very pleasant passage down. General Wall was on board, and is yet quite feeble from a recent stroke of paralysis....*
>
> *The houses at the Island are very full; we got in however at Congress Hall—the aristocratic establishment—and are doing pretty well. I have already met several acquaintances, and made as many more....*
>
> *Frank Johnson gave a Concert to-night in our dining room. The music was good and the audience quite brilliant. Afterwards we had some fireworks, and about midnight a serenade from Frank's band.*[137]

Frank Johnson was a Black master musician, bandleader, composer and arranger in the early to mid-nineteenth century. He was a popular performer who played across other states and in England.[138] Mickle continued his account of his trip:

> *19 July, Wednesday. Cape May.*
>
> *People hardly know what to do with themselves at Cape May, after all its fame as a place of amusement. The bathing is very good, but even the most enthusiastic bather would want to come out occasionally and get dry. To fill up the intervals they have a billiards room or two and several ten pin alleys. You may also pick up shells if you can find any, eat, and look at the women. I tried all these to-day, but without complete success. I was glad when night arrived with a change of employment.*
>
> *This change we had at Congress Hall, in what is technically called "a hop," that is a sociable dance, in the main saloon. It lasted until midnight, longer than which not even Frank Johnson's admirable music could keep them together. The prettiest girl and the best dancer in the room was Miss McKnight of Bordentown.*
>
> *Visitors are still pouring down; and to night I and four others slept in the reading room. I have never seen the Island so full.*[139]

On reaching the cape, visitors were struck with the beauty of the seashore town and comforted by all the big city amenities, such as gaslighted street lamps, a telegraph office that connected with Philadelphia and New York City, mail delivery, daily newspapers from large cities and saloons.[140] Carriages driven by Black coachmen could take them to their hotel or ride them around town to their favorite saloon or gambling club.[141] Visitors were thrilled by the "celebrated colored Philadelphia Ice-Creamer" who appeared out of nowhere and bellowed the flavors in a manner guests relished, imitating or heckling him back.[142] Everything was done to benefit and indulge the guests.

What's Cooking

Harriet Tubman's hegira moment came on September 17, 1849.[143] This was the time to take her freedom. She fled Maryland's Eastern Shore with the help of abolitionist Quakers and landed in the City of Brotherly

Love—Philadelphia—in October. Although she began her quest alone, she was undeterred. Putting her faith in the Lord, she followed the North Star through strange territory, walking at night and staying hidden during the day. Tubman stated, "I had reasoned this out in my mind; there was one of two things I had a *right* to, liberty, or death; if I could not have one, I would have the other; for no man should take me alive; I should fight for my liberty as long as my strength lasted."[144] Tubman's favorite spiritual was "Swing Low Sweet Chariot," which she sang during her flight and was reportedly sung at her funeral. The spiritual's words refer to the Old Testament stories of Elijah and Ezekiel, in which the chariot takes the morally just to heaven. The chariot represents a form of transportation or a conductor on the UGRR, while "Jordan" could mean the North or Canada.[145]

Tubman ran because she found out that her mother should have been freed by her current master under the terms of the former master's will which would also have freed her children. This news was kept from her mother by her current owner. Tubman also became concerned that she would be traded away from her family after her owner died.[146] These things, along with her strong sense of self-worth and purpose, spurred her quest for freedom. W.E.B. Du Bois argued that running away not only was a function that relieved Black people from the labor and cruelty of slavery, it was also a form of action against the idea that someone else could own your body and mind. In essence, it was an act against the institution itself.[147] Runaway slaves denied their owners the financial benefits of their labor in the present and in the future. This was something Tubman instinctively understood. Tubman had the youth, vigor, stamina, spontaneity and fearlessness to risk her life for her goal.

Once her owner discovered she was gone, a fifty-dollar bounty was placed on her head if found in Maryland and one hundred if found out-of-state.[148] Tubman's biographer wrote, "The close espionage under which these poor creatures dwelt, engendered in them a cunning and artifice, which to them seemed only a fair and right attempt on their part, to cope with power and cruelty constantly in force against them."[149] On finally reaching freedom land, Tubman said, "I felt like I was in Heaven." Yet she also felt alone, since there was no one there to share her joy and the rest of her family was still enslaved.[150] In order to help them escape, Tubman needed money, so she took jobs working in private homes, clubhouses and hotels in Philadelphia.[151]

Tubman also reached out to the Philadelphia Vigilance Committee, an antislavery organization where conductor William Still worked, to connect with its members and join the cause. Tubman was introduced to the UGRR

Harriet Tubman, fugitive slave, abolitionist, UGRR conductor, spy, nurse. *Courtesy of Library of Congress*.

through her own experience fleeing Maryland, where she received assistance from abolitionists. This experience brought her into contact with two of the most important conductors in the Delaware Valley: Thomas Garrett and William Still.[152] Garrett was the leading figure working the Wilmington, Delaware UGRR routes. A Quaker, he was a follower of nationally known abolitionist William Lloyd Garrison. By 1861, Garrett had helped over two thousand fugitives during his thirty years of service.[153] Garrett owned a shoe store in Delaware, from which he provided fugitives with footwear before passing them along to the next station.[154] His positioning there was consequential and artful. Wilmington was a major UGRR site because it was the last stop before entering a free state. Garrett's experience and knowledge in UGRR tactics was enormously helpful to Tubman after he assisted her in her freedom flight. He later became aware of Tubman's successful rescue trips during the years 1849 to 1852 and contacted her about working with the UGRR.[155] They became close friends over the years, no doubt due to their shared compassion and commitment to the antislavery cause. Teaming up with these two major UGRR operators, Garrett and Still, made Tubman unstoppable. Together, they could lend her their experience, intelligence and deep knowledge of best practices of this secretive network. Tubman was tutored by superior directors.

In December 1850, Tubman began her rescue trips back south to bring out her sister and her two children. A few months later, she returned to Maryland and rescued a brother and two other men. In the fall, she returned to get her husband, but he refused to go, so she took others instead. In December 1851, she went back and brought out eleven slaves, conducting them to Canada because of the Fugitive Slave Law of 1850, which gave no sanction to runaways except on British soil.[156] It was from these trips that she earned the moniker Moses. As a result of the successfulness of her rescues, slave owners in Maryland grew frantic and set up large rewards for her capture. This led her to perform only two rescues between 1852 and 1857 there, with the last one to bring out her parents.[157] The price on Tubman's head ranged from $12,000, offered by the Maryland legislature, to a total of $40,000, combining all rewards from slave owners and the state.[158]

So with very successful rescue operations already on her record and employment in Philadelphia, why would Tubman feel the need to go to Cape May during the summers? After all, Philadelphia hotels remained open during the summer season. One reason could be that Cape May was a bustling tourist town and playground for elites like Clay who not only came to relax but also took time for business. Clay was the father of compromises to protect slavery and one of the founders of the American Colonization Society (ACS), which promoted sending free Blacks to relocate in Africa but was opposed to ending slavery. While on vacation on the cape, Clay made his headquarters in Congress Hall.[159] As an ACS founder, Clay spoke to the society's members at its annual meetings. Addressing the ACS in 1848, Clay said,

> *We did not intend to do more or less than establish on the shores of Africa a colony, to which free colored persons with their own voluntary consent might go....Far, very far, was it from our purpose to interfere with the slaves, or to shape or affect the title by which they are held in the least degree whatever. We saw and were fully aware of the fact that the free White race and the colored race never could live together on terms of equality.*[160]

In New Jersey, the ACS established an auxiliary chapter, the New Jersey Colonization Society (NJCS), in 1824 on the campus of Princeton University. Many prominent residents of the state were members, including James S. Green (vice president), Dr. John T. Woodhull (vice president) and General John Frelinghuysen, to name a few. The NJCS strongly supported the vision of the ACS.[161]

Into this scene of glamour, wealth, authority and mixing of northern and southern elite appeared Harriet Tubman, the newly escaped slave and Moses of her people. Prestige, power and privilege were the motifs of Cape Island during the summers of the 1850s. It could have seemed like she had stumbled into pharaoh's land, but nothing Tubman did was accidental. In the spring of 1852, Tubman traveled to Cape May to work in hotels and for private families as a cook.[162] Although some historians claim she may have worked there for only one summer, others argue she arrived on the cape earlier and was there up to 1853.[163] No matter when she reached the cape, working at one of the hotels would have positioned her in a location where the constantly changing clientele would not encourage interaction between workers and guests.[164] In an atmosphere like this, she could hear and see without being noticed. As a cook or even a domestic in a hotel, Tubman would have had access to information about all the important guests arriving there. More importantly, as someone who knew how to obtain information from other Blacks, she could have easily gleaned news about prominent people or slave owners from other African American workers or residents and even from the Black slaves brought along to the resort to serve their masters.

As a cook in one of the hotels, she could have been responsible for helping to purchase produce or other types of food at market. Traditionally, this was an important event for African American women and slaves, since going to market permitted these women a space where they could meet, socialize, talk, gossip, exchange news and make money selling goods. This would have been the perfect place for Tubman to gather information seen or overheard by other Black domestics. An added benefit of going to market was that this was not a space White people usually occupied, so groups of Black women congregating would not look out of place.[165] Black cooks were highly valued and given a modicum of respect and authority in the kitchen. "Frederick Law Olmsted, on a visit to a small plantation, observed that the cook did all the planning for meals, as well as the procuring and preparation of the food. The mistress visibly knew little about such matters, which she was happy to leave to her servant," wrote historian Elizabeth Fox-Genovese. "Cooks were respected by the black as well as by the white folks."[166] Plantation mistress Mary Boykin Chesnut spoke to this reliance on cooks in her diary. In an entry dated July 8, 1863, from Portland, Alabama, she wrote, "Next day, at noon, Hetty, mother's old maid, brought my breakfast to my bedside. Such a breakfast it was!…She is my mother's factotum.…She can do everything better than anyone."[167]

In addition, Black servants were trained to be quiet, obedient and attentive when around Whites. As a result, White people were mostly oblivious to servants in their midst, with exceptions. Chesnut remarked on her servants' demeanor during the assault on Fort Sumter when she was in Charleston on April 13, 1861: "Not by one word or look can we detect any change in the demeanor of these negro servants, Lawrence sits at our door, sleepy and respectful, and profoundly indifferent.…People talk before them as if they were chairs and tables. They make no sign. Are they solidly stupid?"[168] Chesnut grew up with slaves, so she was used to having them always around and directing them. Prior to the Civil War starting, she probably never gave a second thought to what they understood or believed, nor would she have countenanced any negative facial expressions or physical gestures from them. The only reason she took notice at that time was the war and her fear that the slaves might flee or repay their masters for their enslavement. In general, servants in the presence of Whites would have been ignored as they served unless their performance was subpar. Conversations about private or personal issues were conducted and gossip openly discussed and commented on by Whites while in the presence of their servants. This is backed by statements from leading proslavery southerners such as Chancellor William

Harper from South Carolina, who wrote that slaves had no understanding of freedom, love or family. They were stupid, he reasoned.[169] All of these statements belie the real reason slaves never showed emotions—they could not, for their own safety. Slave owners never accepted a slave's display of anything but fear and eager compliance.

Tubman's activities served as a contrast to these views. During the war, while out on scouting expeditions on the Combahee River in South Carolina, Tubman easily moved among White southerners, argued historian Catherine Clinton. Even though Tubman could not read or write, she was able to memorize critical information, which she used to help free slaves and relayed back to Union forces.[170] With so many elite southerners, planters and politicians around Cape Island, there would have been plenty of opportunities to overhear conversations and glean bits of important information. We know that Tubman was a Union spy during the Civil War, but she could have also conducted intelligence for the UGRR while in Cape May. According to author Edwin C. Fishel, intelligence is about acquiring knowledge. It can involve espionage in the form of scouting locations, reconnaissance, interrogation of locals and officials, visual observation and interception of enemy flag messages. A lot of scouting was performed by individuals or small teams inside enemy territory.[171] Cape May before the Civil War was certainly enemy territory. "One imagines that most women who acted as spies did not attract any notice. To do so, of course, meant some degree of failure: a good spy is never remarked upon, never makes the paper," contended historian Lyde Cullen Sizer.[172] Historian Jeffrey M. Dorwart wrote,

> Cape May County was a border region, lying precariously between feuding sections of the country and subject to pressure during the late 1850s from both unionists of the industrial North and secessionists from the southern slave states. A South Carolina secessionist state flag flying defiantly in front of one Cape Island hotel symbolized the fragile geographic and socioeconomic character of New Jersey's southernmost county.[173]

New Jersey's attitude toward slavery was determined in part by its dependence on southern markets and the use of free labor in the state. Southern states were committed to using slave labor, which hindered economic diversification and industrialization.[174] New Jersey began moving away from being mainly an agricultural state to an industrial one around 1850. This change concurred with the growth of immigrant labor. Industrial and manufacturing centers were mainly in the northern and western areas of the state, and by 1860 there were an estimated four thousand manufacturers producing products ranging from shoes and clothing to carriages, harnesses and saddles, much of which was sold down south for the plantation markets.[175] Philadelphia also played a major role in the slave market. City merchants owned most of the shipping vessels that carried cargo to southern ports, and city offices provided many financial services to those regions.[176] Philadelphia also manufactured household goods, produced beer and textiles for the southern market, built Baldwin locomotives used in the South and educated southern students in its medical schools and universities.[177]

New Jersey was also one of two free states to officially consent to the extraction of fugitive slaves after passage of the Fugitive Slave Law of 1850.[178] This law had some very negative provisions for fugitives, including denying them the right to a jury trial, allowing the suspected slave to be put before a commissioner appointed by the courts instead of an ordinary judicial tribunal, paying the commissioner ten dollars for every person turned over to a claimant and five dollars if the person went free and giving federal marshals the power to enlist citizens to help enforce the law—whether or not they wanted to comply.[179]

Although most spies change their identity, for Tubman that would not have been necessary in Cape May, because White society would have rendered her invisible in that setting.[180] Some historians point to Tubman as an excellent example of an escape artist, skilled at assuring people and getting them to trust her. "She typically did not use disguise in her rescues of slaves. Rather, she used fortitude and audacity—driving slaves out of the danger zone in a wagon, in plain daylight, struggling through the swamps and keeping up the morale of the group by threatening to shoot anyone who thought about turning back," argued historian Kathleen De Grave.[181] During the war, Tubman was both spy and organizer of scouts, which required skill at selecting Black people in the community who would follow her and be loyal and not betray her.[182] These skills could have been honed in Cape May.

All these things, taken into consideration—the fact that Cape May was a southern playground in the antebellum period hosting the most famous, rich and powerful planters, politicians and businessmen in the country; it was the resort where many White and Black abolitionists also spent their summers; and it had an active UGRR presence—lend credibility to the idea that Tubman's time there was about more than just finding employment. No other resort in the country at that time served as a place of revelry for such a diverse and influential population of White people. For them, Cape May was the place to be seen, socialize, make connections and flirt. What better place for someone like Tubman to cut her teeth in espionage—and with the backing of master abolitionists such as Garrett and Still, she could have performed magic.

Longitude: Expedient

Most of the cape's Black residents worked in the hotels, private homes and stores on the island. Although small in number, their families became a close-knit group, intermarrying, worshipping and living together in their own communities. Edward Turner, a landowner and farmer, had a connection to the UGRR. He maintained a station on the cape and shuttled fugitives to Snow Hill or other South Jersey stations in his wagon. Tubman most certainly knew Turner and would have been involved with him.[183] Another person Tubman would have had contact with was Stephen Smith, a successful Black Pennsylvania coal and lumber businessman, AME minister, abolitionist, organizer and philanthropist. Smith operated his businesses in Columbia, Pennsylvania, working with his partner and relative, William Whipper.[184] After passage of the Fugitive Slave Law of 1850, the men decided to transport fugitives safely by "designing a secret compartment inside their firm's railroad cars," where runaways could be hidden next to the coal and lumber they shipped. Reportedly, not one of their human passengers was ever discovered.[185] Smith, a wealthy entrepreneur, built a summer home in Cape May in 1846 on Lafayette Street across from the Macedonia Baptist Church. While his home was being built, he also undertook construction of another project—the Banneker House, a Black resort—down the street from his new home. Smith was one of the founders of the Pennsylvania Anti-Slavery Society.[186] He later founded the African Methodist Episcopal church on Franklin Street in Cape May in 1888.[187] Frederick Douglass called Smith the richest Black man in America. Although born into slavery, Smith was able to rise to prominence, but he never forgot his people. According to writer Barbara Dreyfuss, Smith's philanthropy included funding libraries and schools for Blacks and aiding the poor by establishing the first home for aged Black Americans. He also sponsored the Banneker Institute, where Black people could attend lectures, debates and other events that would enrich them, according to Dreyfuss. Members of the Banneker

House of Stephen Smith, abolitionist; Cape May. *Author's photo.*

Institute along with Smith purchased property next door to Smith's Cape May residence and opened a hotel for Black clientele during the Civil War, charging Philadelphia city dwellers only eight dollars a week for room and board vacations at the beach.[188]

Next door to Macedonia Baptist Church stands the church parsonage, which dates to the 1790s. In the 1800s, it was the preacher's home. In the twenty-first century, the two-story building has been turned into the Harriet Tubman Museum. On a tour of the former parsonage, now museum, in 2020, museum president Lynda Towns disclosed that during renovations, a secret compartment was found under the floorboards in one room. This compartment was large enough for two people to fit inside it. Towns believed that it could have been used to conceal fugitives before conducting them on to the next stop on the UGRR.[189]

Summers on the cape were sometimes rowdy events, particularly with all the southerners around. One incident on July 31, 1850, between White male guests and Black waiters at the New Atlantic House hotel revealed many

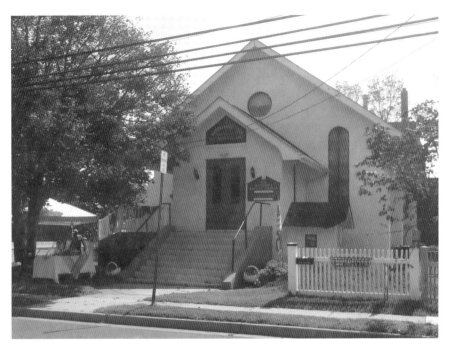

Historic Macedonia Baptist Church, Cape May. *Author's photo*.

Harriet Tubman Museum, Cape May. *Author's photo*.

Left: Lynda Towns, president of the Harriet Tubman Museum, Cape May, 2020. *Author's photo*.

Right: Bob Mullock, chairman of the board, Harriet Tubman Museum, Cape May, 2020, owner & operator of the historic Chalfonte Hotel, Cape May. *Author's photo*.

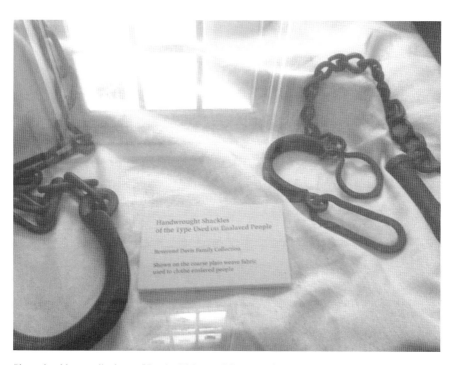

Slave shackles on display at Harriet Tubman Museum, Cape May. *Author's photo*.

things. First, it showed the arrogance and false sense of manhood White southerners held under the idea of chivalry. These men believed they had to exhibit manliness by physical threats and assaults, especially against non-White men and women. In addition, they believed their financial success gave them the right to subjugate others not in their class.[190] Second, the

Opposite: Black doll display at Harriet Tubman Museum, Cape May. *Author's photo*.

Left: Harriet Tubman sculpture by artist Wesley Wofford, at Harriet Tubman Museum, Cape May. *National Park Service*.

incident showed that the Black men involved were not scared of these White men's intimidations and threats and they were willing to fight back.

The incident occurred, reportedly, during a hop at the hotel when a southerner rudely grabbed some refreshments from a tray carried by a Black waiter. The waiter, who may have been taking those drinks to a specific table, commented on the unseemly behavior, which resulted in the White man exclaiming he was "a Southerner of noble blood! And ready for a fight!"[191] The southerner, goaded on by his friends, attacked the waiter. Other Black waiters immediately came to their coworker's defense and assistance as the group of White men also joined the fight, pulling out pistols and daggers. Both the Black and White men received cuts and bruises in the ensuing fight.[192] A rumor spread the next day that the waiters were going to retaliate, and the White females accompanying the southerners persuaded their men to leave that night. This display of Black solidarity did not go over well with the hotel establishment which downplayed the incident to save face and keep the business from suffering backlash from southern patrons. Afterward, the hotel allegedly fired the waiters and played down the melee, but the incident was still written about in a Baltimore newspaper.[193] What is most amazing about this circumstance is not that the southerners threatened Black men and resorted to violence. Rather, the fact that the Black men stood together to repulse an enemy and protect their "brother" is enlightening. They exhibited fearlessness and the desire for revenge by acting precipitously in a manner that not only withstood aggression but also resulted in the Cavaliers quitting the island. It is not known if Tubman was on the Cape at that time or had anything to do with this incident, but it is clear that the abolitionist spirit was manifest in these men's minds and hearts.

Cape May was also a destination for fugitives who braved the open waters of the Delaware Bay. William Still recorded two successful escapes whereby the fugitives landed on the island. In one case, four young men rowed a skiff, a flat-bottomed boat with a shallow draft, across the bay from Lewes, Delaware. Their perilous journey could have ended in tragedy when a strong gale started to blow, creating waves that could have overturned the boat or blown it out to sea. Providence brought the men to shore on Cape May, where there was an oyster boat nearby, and the captain led them to Philadelphia.[194]

Another story involved six fugitives on board a bateau, a lightweight flat-bottomed boat, which shoved off at ten o'clock at night from the Delaware shore near Kitts Hammock. On the open water, the fugitives—Thomas Sipple and his wife, Mary Ann; Henry Burkett and his wife, Elizabeth; John Purnell; and Hale Burton—were attacked by White men in another boat who falsely claimed the boat as theirs and grabbed a chain on the fugitives' boat. The fugitives maintained their right to the boat and resisted the White men's attempts to commandeer it. Violence then erupted between the men in both boats: one White man hit a male fugitive on the head with an oar, breaking it and knocking the Black man down. Thomas Sipple immediately responded, punching one of the White males so hard it sent him crashing down onto the floor of his own boat. The White aggressors panicked and shoved away from the fugitives' boat. Then, at a short distance from the fugitives, the White men pulled out pistols and discharged them at the Black boaters. Many of the fugitives were hit but managed to get away and make it to the Cape May shoreline near the lighthouse. After landing, they solicited the help of a local captain, who brought them to Philadelphia.[195] The Cape May lighthouse these fugitives saw was the second one constructed on the point. Built in 1847, it had a seventy-eight-foot tower located near the site of the present lighthouse, which was constructed in 1859.[196]

After Tubman's death on March 10, 1913,[197] two newspaper notices spoke to her time in Cape May in a very curious manner. According to historian

Cape May lighthouse. *Author's photo.*

Gordon Bond, an obituary stated she "started a settlement at Cape May, New Jersey, in 1852," which was operated in part by Thomas Garrett.[198] Bond also records another account from a newspaper in Tubman's last hometown, Auburn, New York, that contended she had a headquarters at Cape May.[199] It is interesting that these two notices would comment on her time on Cape Island not solely in terms of employment but also as it related to her UGRR activity. Tubman moved into her Auburn home after the Civil War ended. It was obtained for her by President Abraham Lincoln's secretary of state, William H. Seward.[200] Seward was also a staunch abolitionist who participated in the UGRR. He and his wife, Frances Miller Seward, opened their Auburn, New York home to fugitives, hiding them in the basement.[201] Tubman was often a guest in the Seward home as a conductor "forwarding baggage" to Canada, and after the war ended, she continued helping people by providing those in need with a place to stay in her home, according to Christine P. Carter, coordinator of the Harriet Tubman Home in Auburn. Carter's illustration of Tubman's generosity there highlights how fearless, bighearted and unstinted "Moses" could have been while in Cape May, and it also speaks to how connected Tubman was to important abolitionists across the country, which would have provided her with special knowledge of UGRR measures.[202] In later years, Tubman was able to take possession of a twenty-six-acre lot with two houses, which she turned into "an old folks" home. She deeded that property to the AME church in Auburn in 1903.[203]

CHAPTER 4

"THE CAUSE OF AMERICA"

Thomas Paine wrote *Common Sense* in 1776 and addressed it to the people of America. In it, he penned, "The cause of America is in a great measure the cause of all mankind. Many circumstances hath, and will arise, which are not local, but universal, and through which the principles of all Lovers of Mankind are affected, and in the Event of which, their Affections are interested."[204] To Paine, that cause was freedom, independence and self-governance. These same innate ideals were at issue in the antebellum period but were interpreted differently. Southerners wanted the freedom to have slavery anywhere. Many of them agitated for independence from the Union and self-governance in the form of states' rights. Northerners, for the most part, wanted freedom from slavery in new territories or states, independence from the "peculiar institution" in their own states and self-governance free from the aggravating provisions of the Fugitive Slave Law of 1850. In all regards, the cause of America had to do with slavery and free Blacks.

CORRODING EFFORTS

In New Jersey, two organizations worked toward sending American Blacks to Africa as part of their commitment to what they considered the cause of the United States. Instead of making the United States a land of freedom for everyone, they sought to make it one solely for Whites and slavery. In

1816, the Presbyterian Synod of New York and New Jersey approved a resolution to "appoint a Board of Directors to establish and superintend an African School, for the purpose of educating young men of colour, to be teachers and preachers and send them to Africa to educate and preach the gospel to natives."[205]

The organization's intent was to train American Blacks in a school located in Parsippany, New Jersey for this so-called racial uplift, yet, there was also an undercurrent of racism involved since many of the board's directors were advocates of the colonization movement, which proposed sending free Blacks to live in Africa.[206]

The synod was ignorant of the fact that many people on the African continent had knowledge of and practiced established religions. It also disregarded the fact that Africans had civilizations and knowledge of science. Historians John Hope Franklin and Alfred A. Moss Jr. described the various sub-Saharan African empires that existed on the continent before European conquest. Concentrating on West Africa, Franklin and Moss related the military, political and social/cultural systems that existed in the different empires. They argued, based on archaeological and anthropological evidence, that some of those states had advanced kingdoms and civilizations.[207] They maintained that even small states or kingdoms contained some kind of political system of government, arts and literature.[208] Religion was also an important aspect among peoples in West Africa, with many practicing the Christian and Muslim faiths.[209]

Regardless, racists did not view any African civilization as equal to European or American society. So the synod's views made sense to colonization advocates. But the synod made clear—or murky, depending on your view—its stance on slavery. "On the principle of slavery we have nothing to say. We only affirm that America is the greatest receptacle which has received the streams that Africa has discharged. And for this we owe her large arrears."[210] In 1817, the Parsippany School offered Black students a four-year course of study for the purpose of colonization. These courses were open to any Black student who showed aptitude for reading and writing. Another such school was opened in Newark in 1830.[211]

Even though the synod was reluctant to admit its feelings on slavery, the New Jersey chapter of the ACS (NJCS) was not timid at all. On July 14, 1824, it held a meeting in Princeton to form a chapter. Robert Field Stockton, grandson of a signer of the Declaration of Independence (Richard Stockton), was appointed president and chairman. He opened the meeting by stating that Negroes had no stake in American society and its institutions.[212] NJCS member Robert Finley was also a member of the Presbyterian synod who advocated training Blacks so they could go to Africa. Finley told the NJCS that the ACS believed freeing slaves would be dangerous without having a place to send them outside of the United States.[213]

Member James S. Green urged adoption of the NJCS's constitution, stating in part, "What a mass of ignorance, misery and depravity, is here mingled with every portion of our population, and threatening the whole with a moral and political pestilence. My answer then to the State of New-Jersey is, that this enormous mass of revolting wretchedness and deadly pollution will, it is believed, be ultimately taken out of her territory, if the plan of the Colonization Society be adopted."[214] Green stressed that only removal of Blacks from among White Americans could be an option for the state. "Nothing but total amputation will affect a cure," he argued.[215] The ACS, in its *Twenty-Ninth Annual Report*, heralded New Jersey's strong support of the cause and expected a big increase in interest in the state, believing the NJCS would "have a very important influence in arousing the attention of the community to the transcendent importance of the cause it advocates."[216] At the NJCS meeting in Princeton, Green charged that free Blacks had no place in America because they were uncivilized, they were denied entry into White society and institutions and their children were excluded from attending schools alongside White children. He cautioned White residents against using Black servants as domestics or caregivers for White children since those Blacks could secretly harbor hate and do them harm. Green rhetorically asked if education would make Blacks better, answering his own question: "You may make them free, but you make them worthless."[217] Green had a lot to say about free Blacks—all of it negative. He questioned the reasoning behind gradual abolition despite it having been in existence for twenty years. The number of free Blacks had increased to the point that he believed their numbers would make them a threat to Whites, and he argued there would be no legal restraints on them. Green feared that since Blacks had no protection under the law, they would violently oppose the law. He disapproved of any option to grant rights to free Blacks and felt confident that other White people in the state would reject any such suggestion.[218] Green had no better words for slaves, claiming they had nothing to lose by becoming a threat to White society. He stated, "The slave is a mere animal, robbed of all the nobler feelings of our nature, unmoved by the calls of ambition or the suggestions of prudence."[219] Green added, "Call it folly, to be frightened by the word *black*; prejudice to hate a black skin; the mere effect of education to separate this race so widely from ourselves. I admit it all. You must put the blacks by *themselves* and they must make a society of their own, if they are to be real freemen."[220]

The NJCS had reason to believe New Jersey would be fertile ground for its message. New Jersey was the last northern state to abolish slavery, and when it did pass an act to do so, there were conditions that kept slaves bonded until early adulthood, and other laws restricted Black life in every way. In addition, Blacks were regulated to the lowest-paying and hardest jobs. More importantly, New Jersey's elite had a stranglehold over the social and economic situations in the state. Elite White men dominated the upper-level occupations, lived in the better neighborhoods, headed the big corporations and businesses and ran the local and state governmental offices. Elites perpetually intermarried and had family connections going back to Revolutionary War figures, argued historian Philip C. Davis. This figured strongly in opportunities available to those like themselves and restricted those jobs accessible to others. In antebellum society, family connections ruled the day, blocking outsiders and newcomers from breaking through the glass ceiling into their perceived world of power and exclusiveness.[221] Moreover, many of these elite White men also were the backers of colonization.

Their persuasion and advocacy of this plan also intrigued some White South Jersey residents, such as Isaac Mickle, who were interested in learning more about colonization. Mickle attended a lecture in Camden on December 19, 1841, and recorded the experience in his diary: "This evening I went to the Methodist Church with all the town to hear one George Brown, an African Missionary, tell about the degraded state of the Africans. He told some very tough stories." According to the diary's editor, the missionary, G.S. Brown, served in Liberia around 1839–40 and returned to the United States giving speaking tours on behalf of colonization advocates.[222] Upwardly mobile Whites, like Mickle, were more than likely to have prejudicial ideas about Blacks. In his diary, Mickle's tone is one of interest in the plan rather than compassion for Blacks and reflects how other Whites felt, too. In a January 18, 1841 entry, Mickle recounts a discussion he had with a group of his friends over "which have suffered more by the discovery of America, the Indians or the Negroes?" One friend, Samuel Cowperthwaite, believed "a being that has no brains can feel no sufferings; a negro has no brains; therefore a negro can have no sufferings."[223] Mickle called that answer "ingenious sophistry," even though he believed the argument that Blacks suffered the most was more accurate.

Newspapers in the state also ran articles or editorials touting the ACS, supporting slavery or denouncing abolitionists. The *Camden Mail and General Advertiser* ran a brief notice about a colony of Blacks in Upper Canada living on six hundred acres who survived in the cold and contrasted that to how free Blacks here struggled.[224] Editor of the *Trenton True American* newspaper David Naar was a staunchly proslavery Democrat and political leader. He wrote editorials for his paper defending slavery and denouncing Abraham Lincoln during the war, which led to mob violence and threats against supporters of the Union in the state.[225] As the southern states began to secede, Naar reportedly reminded guests at a banquet for the opening of the Erie tunnel in early 1861 that New Jersey had loyally adhered to the U.S. Constitution and the Fugitive Slave Law of 1850 with rendition of fugitives back to their owners. But he cautioned against the government using force to prevent the South from leaving the Union. He argued that secession was a done deal and New Jersey had better wise up. "There must be no coercion; the south had gone, and without her New York would be [no] more than a fishing village, and New Jersey but little better."[226]

According to historian Charles Merriam Knapp, the *Newark Journal* published two propaganda letters to sway readers across the state to side with the Confederacy. In the two letters, written between former New Jersey governor Rodman M. Price and one L.W. Burnett, the correspondents speak on secession. In the first letter, Burnett asked Price whether he believed there will be two confederacies and what would be New Jersey's part. Price replied, "I believe the Southern Confederacy permanent" and predicted that the remaining states would side with the North pertaining to the lost trade and employment for residents who made products for the southern market. Price theorized foreign markets would take over those southern markets, depriving Americans of that profit. As a result, New Jersey would become poor, and its agriculture would be detrimentally affected. Burnett then asked Price who would advise the state on how to maintain its honor. Price replied that the states of New York and Pennsylvania would side with New Jersey once the true dangers to their markets became apparent. Price added that New Jersey should be the first to hold out its hand of reconciliation to the South. "We believe that slavery is no sin; that Slavery—subordination to the superior race—is his [the Caucasian's] natural and normal condition," Price stated.[227] The former governor urged a change to the U.S. Constitution codifying slavery as the only way to save the country.[228]

The ACS had the ear of many Whites. As a result, the needs and concerns of lower-class residents and Blacks were not important matters. Their efforts to deport free Blacks did not hinge on bad actions or real threats to them by freedmen but solely on racism, hiding behind an ostensible desire to give liberty to Blacks. The ACS utilized clergy and educators to promote its cause, cloaking itself in probity, all the while providing a deceitful alternative to life in the United States yet never challenging or addressing the inhumanity of slavery.

CHAPTER 5

"THE SUN NEVER SHINED
ON A CAUSE OF GREATER WORTH"

The sun never shined on a cause of greater worth." Thomas Paine wrote that sentence in *Common Sense* about America's cause of freedom during the Revolution. He reasoned this was the moment for colonists to remain united with faith and honor in their American fight for independence and liberty. He also warned that the slightest rupture in unity and support for the cause would be like carving a name into a young tree trunk: the engraving would continue to expand and affect the tree for the rest of its life.[229] To abolitionists, slavery's demise was the cause that was worth one's life, and they rationalized that if they did not fight the beast, slavery, it would eat away at freedom for all just like carving into a tree.

Du Bois wrote, "As long as there was a slave in America, America could not be a free republic; and more than that: as long as there were people in America, slaves or nominally free, who could not participate in government and industry and society as free, intelligent human beings, our democracy had failed of its greatest mission."[230]

SALTSHAKERS

The ACS's façade of Black uplift was really a front to exile free Blacks from the United States. Historian Clement A. Price argued that because the ACS and the NJCS cloaked their efforts in Christian charity, many White residents found their argument appeasing to their minds and souls. But Blacks in New Jersey viewed that movement as a threat to their quest for freedom, equality and desire for citizenship. As a result, few Blacks in the state took the ACS up on its offer to colonize them in Liberia, Africa. The ACS and NJCS advocated for the voluntary removal of free Blacks from the United States for resettlement in ACS-established colonies in Africa. The purpose was to achieve a total evacuation of all Blacks from the country, except for those enslaved. Beginning in the 1840s, Black residents of New Jersey requested the state legislature not to finance ACS ventures. Black ministers Samuel E. Cornish, a Newark Presbyterian pastor, and Theodore S. Wright, a graduate of Princeton Theological Seminary, denounced colonization as an implement of the slave system.[231]

Despite those efforts, New Jersey received petitions from colonization supporters to finance the ACS plan. Price stated that legislators complied by making annual appropriations of $1,000 every year from 1852 to 1859 to remove free Blacks to Liberia. According to Price, in 1838, the NJCS collected enough funds to establish a town on the west coast of Africa, to be named New Jersey.[232] In its *Twenty-Ninth Annual Report*, the ACS recognized how strong the NJCS's commitment was through the number of people contributing to its cause and noted that the state's residents were well informed about the ACS's plan. As a result, the ACS was expecting a major increase in membership or contributions, especially since NJCS member and honorary manager Rev. Dr. Archibald Alexander was about to publish his *History of Colonization*, which the society believed would increase interest in its cause.[233]

In 1830, abolitionists and free Blacks held a convention in Philadelphia to discuss colonization efforts and schools being formed offering free education to Black students in preparation for colonization. The group agreed to oppose educating their children at these schools and expressed fears that they were really indoctrination centers to ready their children for exile in Africa. The convention also urged Blacks to raise themselves up in this country through hard work and study in educational programs that would help them succeed in America.[234]

Abolitionist writer Lydia Maria Child faulted the ACS for deceiving the public about slavery and for covering up its failures. She targeted NJCS member James S. Green in particular for his statement that slaves were treated with "kindness" and "little cruelty" by slave owners. Critically, she wrote: "In their constitution they have pledged themselves not to speak, write, or do anything to offend the Southerners; and as there is no possible

Lydia Maria Child, abolitionist, writer. *Courtesy of Library of Congress.*

way of making the truth pleasant to those who do not love it, the Society must perforce keep the truth out of sight. In many of their publications, I have thought I discovered a lurking tendency to palliate slavery; or at least to make the best of it."[235]

Child, a Massachusetts Quaker, detested slavery and assisted fugitives in their freedom quest. She admitted that sometimes evil can have an appealing appearance, "But slavery is all evil—within and without—root and branch,—bud, blossom, and fruit!"[236] Other abolitionists also criticized proponents of colonization. In the December 1847 issue of the *North Star*, Frederick Douglass wrote an open letter to Henry Clay criticizing his record of compromise toward slavery and colonization stating, "We live here—have lived here—have a right to live here, and mean to live here."[237]

Blacks in New Jersey during the 1840s and 1850s did not just sit back and accept inequality. Intelligent Black leaders expressed the community's grievances and concerns to public officials. According to Price, in 1849,

Black residents from two South Jersey counties, Salem and Gloucester, called on the state legislature to take away voting restrictions against Blacks in the state.[238] In the antebellum period, New Jersey restricted voting rights to only White males, but these voting restrictions did not always exist. In 1776, the first state constitution allowed voting by anyone who met the property requirements. This might have been an oversight by those legislators that was done without consideration of the implications. As a result, women, Negroes and aliens were permitted voting rights under the law, and many took advantage of that privilege. This happened because the constitution failed "to specify *white* male citizens" only.[239] The state rectified its mistake in 1807 by revoking the franchise for free Blacks and women.[240]

The 1844 constitution also caused a controversy pertaining to Blacks. Legal expert Gary K. Wolinetz argued that Article 1 in the constitution quoted the resounding principles of the Declaration of Independence: "All men are by nature free and independent, and have certain natural and unalienable rights, among which are those of enjoying and defending life and liberty, acquiring, possessing, and protecting property, and of pursuing and obtaining safety and happiness."

Abolitionists focused on this article to bolster their claim that it supported the argument for liberty to slaves still in bondage in the state. This led to a case that went before the state supreme court—*State v. Post*—with abolitionists arguing that the "1844 Constitution abolished slavery and the involuntary servitude of slave children." But the New Jersey Supreme Court ruled otherwise, stating that the 1844 constitution did not affect slavery or involuntary servitude.[241]

After the legislature disregarded their pleas, sixteen African American leaders organized two statewide conventions in 1849, which were held in Trenton.[242] Gloucester County resident Henry Dickerson was selected to be a delegate at the second convention. Dickerson was born in Maryland and moved with his wife, Sophia, and their children to Philadelphia in the 1830s but decided to leave the city because of mob violence against Blacks. The family settled in Woodbury in the 1840s and joined Bethel AME Church, becoming involved in church functions and in community activism. Dickerson participated as a member of the church's correspondence committee at the second convention along with another county resident, Robert Stewart of Woolwich, who also played a part.[243] These conventions were the first for Black people in the state. Despite their efforts, state legislators were not open to the convention's demands. The conventioneers then decided to take their case to the people of New Jersey.

Three South Jersey ministers—Joshua Woodlin of Burlington, W.T. Catto of Trenton and Ismael Locke of Camden—submitted their appeal, *An Address to the Citizens of New Jersey*, directly to the people, hoping they would protest. Black people across the state, including some from Gloucester, Salem and Cumberland Counties, petitioned the state legislature to address the issues of suffrage for Black men and equality, but the state also ignored those calls for action.[244]

"New Jersey has never treated us like men. She has always been an ardent supporter of the 'peculiar institution'—the watchdog for the Southern plantations," wrote John S. Rock in 1849.[245] Rock was born on October 13, 1825, in Salem County, New Jersey, according to the African American Registry.[246] His hometown was in Elsinboro Township, located below Salem City.[247] This area was where many Blacks lived, worshipped and where some of the most ardent abolitionists in the county came from, including poet Esther "Hetty" Saunders and Reverend/UGGR conductor Thomas Clement Oliver. Saunders, a fugitive slave from Delaware, was brought to the area by her father, who persuaded another family, Joseph and Ann Hall, to care for her when slave catchers arrived looking for them. Esther lived with the Halls after her father fled and even when he returned, while Oliver grew up on a Quaker farm in the township.[248] Living and growing up in this rural South Jersey abolitionist-strong area surely affected Blacks, including the Rock family. Rock showed himself to be precocious at an early age. His parents, John and Maria, recognized his intelligence and had the wherewithal to seek out ways to quench his

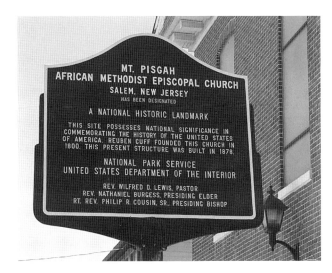

Sign, historic Mt. Pisgah AME Church, Salem. *Author's photo.*

Above: Church bell from the original 1840s Bethel AME Church, Woodbury, outside the present edifice. *Author's photo*.

Left: Historic Mt. Pisgah AME Church, Salem, front view. *Author's photo*.

Historic Mount Pisgah AME Church Cemetery, Elsinboro, Salem County. *Author's photo.*

appetite for learning by enrolling him in the Salem Quaker School for Black students. Rock excelled, and at age eighteen, he started teaching at the school; he became headmaster in 1845.[249]

In South Jersey, the Salem and Haddonfield Quaker Monthly Meetings used interest on funds to finance education for poor White and Black students. In 1803, the Haddonfield School had at least eighty children attending. Students were taught, among other subjects, Latin, mathematics, French and geography. Members of the Society of Friends could also establish a student's education or fund education in general by making a bequest in their will.[250] In 1777, the Salem Quakers began raising money for books and a Black school.[251]

During the same time he was serving as headmaster, Rock also began studying medicine under Salem physicians Drs. Quinton Gibbon and Jacob Sterne Thompson-Sharp. Despite Rock's intense study and educational excellence, racism prevented him from being accepted into medical school in New Jersey. Instead of dwelling on that rejection, Rock turned his attention and concentration to studying dentistry, becoming an apprentice under Dr. Samuel C. Harbert. In 1849, he completed his study, and the next year, he opened a dental practice in Philadelphia. While in Philadelphia, he was able to attend classes at the American College of Medicine, earning a medical degree in 1852 or 1853.[252] It was during this time that his involvement in the abolition movement first began, when he spoke at the Twelfth Annual Meeting of the Pennsylvania Anti-Slavery Society. This gathering inspired him so much that he started publishing articles on abolition in Philadelphia

1800s schoolhouse owned and operated by historic Bethel AME Church, Woodbury. *Author's photo.*

1800s student desk from the historic schoolhouse, Bethel AME Church, Woodbury. *Author's photo.*

Dr. Samuel Harbert's dental office, Salem, where John Rock apprenticed. *Author's photo*.

newspapers.[253] Rock also participated in the Colored Convention held in 1849, serving as secretary and lecturer.[254] In an 1850 speech directed at White New Jersey residents, Rock addressed Black suffrage. In this speech, which was published in the *North Star*, he challenged Whites to consider and question how newly arrived immigrants could be more knowledgeable about U.S. government and regulations and more qualified for the right to vote than Blacks who had lived here all their lives. "There is no just plea, and apology for you to shut every avenue to elevation, and then complain of degradation; what also can *be* expected, while we are looked upon as *things*, and treated worse than unthinking animals?"[255] Rock promoted racial pride, unity and free will. He was an early advocate of Black pride and militancy, which inspired protestors in the twentieth century long before the Black Power movement of the 1960s.[256]

Unfortunately for the South Jersey African American community, in 1853, Rock moved to Boston for better opportunities and began studying law. He passed the Massachusetts bar in 1861, then opened a practice there. He later became the first Black man to argue a case before the U.S. Supreme Court, in 1865, and the first Black man to "be received on the floor during a session of the United States House of Representatives," according to historians James Oliver Horton and Lois E. Horton.[257]

Rock may have moved to Boston to further his academic and professional life, but his creative and intellectual acumen and desire to help his people was honed and perfected by his experiences in South Jersey. The Quaker influence and active Black resistance in South Jersey molded his thinking and beliefs about abolition. It is probable that Rock would not have become such a compassionate and articulate voice for Black suffrage, civil rights and liberty if he had been born and raised outside of the South Jersey/Philadelphia/Wilmington area—part of the Delaware Valley region. This area was among some exceptional northern regions, such as New Bedford and Boston, Massachusetts, that had aggressively strong White and Black abolitionist support. The Quaker influence here allowed Rock to thrive and grow. He obtained many opportunities because of those Quaker connections and sympathetic feelings toward Blacks. In addition, the fact that there were other strong Black families in the area who defied slavery also had an effect on Rock's self-actualization and the development of his racial pride.

ROCK SALT SUPPORT

On March 4, 1861, Abraham Lincoln was inaugurated as the sixteenth president of the United States. One month after his election win, the South Carolina state convention held a vote on December 20, 1860, to secede from the Union. It passed. Over the next month, six other southern states also followed South Carolina's lead.[258] The implications of these actions reached across the states. In New Jersey, half of Princeton University's student population left school and returned to their southern homes to prepare to fight for the Confederacy.[259] Once the first act of southern aggression occurred with the taking of Fort Sumter, New Jersey residents were compelled to take sides. As residents in the state reeled, many state legislators stood fast in support of the South. Although Democratic politicians and even the governor advocated for seeking peace with the South by compromise, one New Jersey legislator opposed the proslavery factions of the state, defended the Lincoln administration's policies and advocated for Black equality. In 1862, James M. Scovel was elected to the state legislature for District 1, Camden County, as a Republican. When the state house of assembly considered joint resolutions concerning the "Peace Resolutions," Scovel vehemently denounced them, stating in part:

We now stand at the very crisis of our fate. If we are bold and vigilant and active, the good ship will weather the storm. But we hear threats of revolution in the North. From whom? From that tender party of peace, who chose to be partisans to do Jefferson Davis' bidding, rather than be patriots on the side of the Union.

God takes care of his universe, and while we cannot understand all the problems which surround this momentous and terrible struggle, it is enough for us to know that God's purpose is over it all, and that these peace patriots may as well hold up their printed resolutions before the lightnings of heaven as to stay the tide of this righteous war. We must meet the Slavery question like men.[260]

Scovel disputed arguments from the proslavery side that he and others were trying to take the country away from White people. Instead, he maintained, they only wanted rights for Black people. "My creed on this question is simply this, all things should be subordinate to the Union. If slavery stands in the way of the Union, let it share the fortunes or the fate of war."[261]

The Peace Resolutions came out of fears over secession. On January 8, 1861, New Jersey governor Charles S. Olden (Republican, 1860–63) addressed the state senate and assembly on several issues, including southern secession threats. Olden essentially agreed with the South on its reasoning for secession and blamed abolitionists for agitation. Olden asserted the state was blameless concerning its commitment to laws, stating:

That the non-slaveholding states have not recognized, been bound by or obeyed the supreme law of the land—the Constitution and the laws made under it, viz: the Fugitive Slave law and the decisions of the Supreme Court. Second—That the citizens of the slave states are by the others denied equal rights in the territories. The first of these charges addresses itself to the states in their separate capacity, and in that aspect we propose to meet it. Since the adoption of the constitution, New Jersey has, with a faithfulness that has never been questioned, excepting through ignorance, fulfilled every obligation assumed under its provisions, fully, fairly and distinctly. The laws on our statute books in relation to fugitives were enacted for the purpose of facilitating their rendition to their owners....The decisions of the Supreme Court have ever been held by New Jersey as the law of the land, and we trust ever will, whether distasteful or not.[262]

He added:

> *Most of the differences that set people and nations at variance could be adjusted if the fear of compromising what is called "honor" did not deter each from making concessions. It requires more courage to acknowledge and make reparation than to persist—more to yield than to fight....Let us hope that the representatives of all the states at Washington will rise above such fears—above the temper that vents itself by spiteful actions and opprobrious epithets, and act with an eye single to the welfare of the whole country.*
>
> *The great mass of the people in all sections, we are thankful to believe, are strongly attached to the Union; a majority of the southern states, and those most exposed to the evils connected with the agitation of slavery, are still standing with us in favor of the Union. To those true-hearted patriots we owe much, and let us strengthen their hands by a disposition to conciliate and yield to all proper demands.*[263]

Olden also approved of sending delegates to attend what was called the Peace Convention. The governor and nine other elite White men from New Jersey made up the state's Peace Convention delegates—Olden, P.D. Vroom, R.F. Stockton, B. Williamson, Jos. F. Randolph, F.T. Frelinghuysen, R.M. Price, Wm. C. Alexander and T.J. Stryker. They met with delegates from twenty-one other states at the Willard Hotel in Washington, D.C., from February 4 through February 27, 1861, to discuss resolutions to maintain the Union. The convention delegates agreed on seven propositions that would, on ratification by the states, become amendments to the U.S. Constitution. The proposals brought back to the states conceded to the South virtually everything it wanted.[264] The fact that at least two of the New Jersey delegates were NJCS officers, two were former Democratic governors and the rest, except for Olden, were Democrats is very telling of the group's intentions. That these delegates thought their resolutions would satisfy abolitionists in the North is bewildering, yet the commissioners believed all the states would ratify the proposals.

The proposed amendments to the Constitution brought back to New Jersey included seven sections:

> *Section 1 prohibited slavery above the 36° 30' north latitude except as a crime, but allowed it below that latitude;*
>
> *Section 2 only allowed new territory to be acquired by a majority vote of senators from both free and slave states;*

100

Section 3 prohibited any new amendments to the U.S. Constitution to abolish slavery or interfere with it in any state, territory, or area it existed;

Section 4 prohibited states from using the parts of the Constitution to prevent enforcement of the fugitive slave act;

Section 5 prohibited foreign slave trade in the U.S. or its territories;

Section 6 prohibited amending parts of the Constitution without consent of all the states; and

Section 7 required by law that the U.S. government compensate slave owners the full value of fugitive slaves who were not apprehended due to violence, intimidation, or any other acts.[265]

When the state legislature considered the Peace Resolutions, Scovel cautioned against passing them, saying:

Discarding all personal feeling, if I ever entertained any, and recognizing in many of them the social virtues which adorn society, I cannot but regard, with rare exceptions, the leaders of the dominant party in New Jersey as enemies of their Government and false to their country.[266]

Scovel then excoriated the proposals, stating:

For these many years slavery has been working evil under the sun. Bench and bar, and hall and pulpit, and counting room, and field and fireside, have been tainted with its presence. It has tampered with public and private honesty. It has debased, degraded and brutalized American freemen, marring their birthright. It has turned their beautiful garden into a wilderness. The ignorance that disgraces, the vice that demoralizes, the barrenness that lays waste the South, are all its work.[267]

Slavery mocked the country, he said, and he could no longer defend it as he had previously. "But I was not willing that the slave power should assume the place of the government, and that all the interests of the country should be made subservient to it," he said, and he could not abide the Democratic Party becoming a lackey to slave owners.[268] Despite his best efforts, the legislature approved the Peace Resolutions anyway.

An incident involving the state legislature underscored the body's partisanship. This incident should have made all the legislators angry, but it did not. On March 10, 1863, Scovel presented a report made by a committee appointed to look into where a U.S. flag that hung in the assembly chamber had gone and who removed it. The committee could not determine who removed the flag or where it was presently, but it did learn that the flag had been used "to grace a 'copperhead' funeral" at a secession committee meeting held at the Girard House in Philadelphia.[269] No action was taken by the assembly, and the report was tabled after being read. The reason may have been that the New Jersey legislature was majority Democratic, pro-South and proslavery. Also indicative of the legislature's proslavery sympathy and apathy toward Blacks is the fact that other than the committee that investigated the flag's disappearance, no one put up a resolution to denounce the incident or further inquire into who could have removed the flag, although the theft was a breach of the reverence of the assembly chamber and an insult to the United States because the flag was used as part of a copperhead cohort.

Those copperhead members made their feelings known in various ways, such as proposing resolutions or bills in March to prohibit Negroes or "mulattos," other than those already here, from entering or settling in the state.[270] The assembly passed the bill on March 18, 1863, by a thirty-three to twenty vote. It prevented Black immigration into the state and also defined Blacks' status. During the debate, Bergen County assemblyman Thomas Dunn English argued that this bill was for the benefit of South Jersey, although historian Charles Merriam Knapp contended that only two South Jersey representatives voted for the bill and both of them were Democrats.[271] According to Knapp, the bill called for any Negro or "mulatto" who came into the state and remained longer than ten days to be deemed guilty of a misdemeanor and, if convicted, transported to Liberia or the West Indies. In addition, anyone found bringing such people into the state or found harboring them would be punished by fines or imprisonment. The state senate read the bill but did not take action on it. Knapp argued that this was an attempt to "nullify in part the Emancipation Proclamation" by excluding free Blacks from the state.[272] This bill was also intended to target abolitionists in South Jersey who were assisting fugitives in their freedom quest, so if the bill had passed both chambers, more pressure would have been put on abolitionists, and freedmen and immigrants risked being forced into colonization if convicted.

Copperheads were sometimes called Peace Democrats because they supported the South's proslavery stance and opposed the Lincoln administration's attempts to reunite the nation during the Civil War.[273] Peace Democrats were also called copperheads by Republican newspapers because they wore lapel pins made from copper pennies.[274]

After Fort Sumter fell, antiwar residents across the state began holding peace meetings, particularly in Cumberland County in South Jersey and Bergen County in North Jersey.[275] Once fighting began, David Naar, the outspoken copperhead, exclaimed, "We are cutting each other's throats for the sake of a few worthless negroes."[276] Copperheads in the state legislature opposed emancipation in March 1863 as part of their antiwar effort. This stance caught the attention of two White New Jersey regiments stationed in Virginia. The soldiers were so upset over this action that they sent letters of resolution to the legislature calling the Peace Resolutions "wicked weak and cowardly" and those supporting them traitors. Although the copperhead influence in the state legislature fell away over time, Democrats still remained in control.[277]

After Lincoln issued the Emancipation Proclamation, some influential people, such as Peter Cooper, co-owner of the Trenton Iron Company—which produced iron rails for the Camden and Amboy Railroad and, by 1850, was the largest iron producer—understood Lincoln's intent and appreciated the effect it was having on slaves and slave owners.[278] In a letter to New York Democratic governor Horatio Seymour, Cooper related a conversation he had with Mr. Dean, provost-marshal of St. Louis, to the effect that the proclamation had weakened the rebel cause more than anything else and that captured rebel officers admitted it as well. In addition, he stated that rebel officers and Negroes knew about the proclamation five days before other Whites did.[279] Now seventy-three years old, Cooper admitted to being a lifelong Democrat who always fell in line with the party position. His military experience serving in the War of 1812 had given him more perspective and the right to speak his mind about the dangers to the United States from the Democratic stance on slavery. Cooper asserted his belief that "it does now, it always has, and will forever, require the united powers of all the states to hold securely the dear-bought treasure of freedom and independence a treasure that should be the pride and glory of every American citizen."[280] He criticized those individual states that maintained they had their own sovereignty. Quoting James Madison from the Constitutional Convention, Cooper wrote, "The states never possessed the essential right of sovereignty. These were always vested in Congress."[281] Cooper reminded Seymour that President Lincoln, as commander-in-chief of the army and navy, had "use of all the powers of the nation, to preserve its interests, its honor, and its life."[282]

This reminder was a not-so-subtle quip about Seymour's lack of response to New York's Draft Riots in the summer of 1863. According to historian

Walter A. McDougall, Seymour was a "notorious copperhead" who was elected to New York's governor's office in 1862.[283] Those Draft Riots were the result of two things happening in the city: competition between White workers and Irish immigrants against Blacks for jobs and the government drafting immigrants and unemployed White men for military service in the Civil War. These Whites resented conscription and resisted it, since they viewed the war as being waged just to set Blacks free. In the July riots, Black homes, businesses and organizations were burned; Black men, women and children were injured and killed; and even some White homes were burned.[284]

Union army surgeon Dr. John Gardner Perry experienced the fear and wrath of those rioters beginning on July 20, 1863, while recuperating in his New York City residence from an army-related injury. Perry stated he had no idea he and his wife were in danger. He wrote:

> On the first day of the riot, in the early morning, I heard loud and continued cheers at the head of the street, and supposed it must be news of some great victory. In considerable excitement I hurried downstairs to hear particulars, but soon found that the shouts came from the rioters who were on their way to work. About noon that same day we became aware of a confused roar; as it increased, I flew to the window, and saw rushing up Lexington Avenue, within a few paces of our house, a great mob of men, women, and children; the men in red working shirts, looking fairly fiendish as they brandished clubs, threw stones, and fired pistols. Many of the women had babies in their arms, and all of them were completely lawless as they swept on.[285]

Perry sat next to a window to watch the mobs and, without thinking, he threw over his shoulders his military coat, which displayed military shoulder straps which, if noticed, could have resulted in him being shot by a rioter out of anger against the army. "The mass of humanity soon passed, setting fire to several houses quite near us, for no other reason, we heard afterward, then that a policeman, whom they suddenly saw and chased, ran inside one of the gates, hoping to find refuge. The poor man was almost beaten to death, and the house, with those adjoining, burned."[286]

All night long, Perry heard rioting and from his roof witnessed the city, illuminated by five fires, burning. The next day, he saw even worse actions. "The next day was a fearful one. Men both colored and White, were murdered within two blocks of us, some being hung to the nearest lamp-post, and others shot. An Army officer was walking in the street near our house, when a rioter was seen to kneel on the sidewalk, take aim, fire, and kill him, then coolly start on his way unmolested."[287] Rioting and violence continued all day and night until the third day. Early that morning, Perry found his Black servants all scared and heard the news that rioters were murdering any Black person they came upon. One servant recounted a terrifying story of going outside to clean the front door only to have several Irish people swear and threaten her while accusing Black people of being the cause of all the trouble. It was then that Perry decided to try to get everyone out of the house, but it was too late to do so safely. Instead, his wife's brothers came and told him they would go get help. The brothers returned with a group of cops and citizens vowing to protect their neighborhoods. This group saved the Perrys' home from being burned. The next day, Perry finally felt at ease. "By this time the city was full of troops, and finally the riot was quelled by firing canisters into the mob," he wrote.[288]

During the rioting, Seymour never called out police from across the state to come protect the city and quell any violence. It took the federal government sending in troops to restore calm. Cooper argued in his letter that slavery was destroying the country and the war was opening the door to foreign intervention. He maintained that if the government continued to "perpetuate an institution that enables thousands to sell their own children to be enslaved, with all their posterity," the nation would collapse.[289] The draft riots in New York spilled over into New Jersey but on a smaller scale. Several New Jersey towns experienced rioting, including Newark, which saw the *Mercury* newspaper office vandalized because of its pro-war stance, and the home of Provost Marshall Miller was also stoned.[290]

While the Peace Conference met, Lincoln had already embarked on his approximately two-thousand-mile cross-country trip preceding his inauguration. The president-elect's journey took him to the state capitals in Indiana, Ohio, New York, Pennsylvania, New Jersey and several others, as a gesture of reassurance to southerners and their supporters that his election did not present a threat to the South's institutions of slavery. But he insisted that the South could not break the Union. To him, secession was "anarchy," and Lincoln observed that the Constitution was older than most of the states that threatened to secede. Lincoln earlier argued, "Having never been States, either in substance, or in name, *outside* the Union, whence this magical omnipotence of 'States rights,' asserting a claim of power to lawfully destroy the Union itself?"[291]

Lincoln arrived in New Jersey in February 1861, receiving an official welcome in Jersey City. From there, he traveled to Newark for a reception.[292]

On February 21, Lincoln stopped in Trenton to address a joint session of the state senate and general assembly. Standing before the legislature, he paid homage to New Jersey's Revolutionary War history and how, as a child, he read about Washington crossing the Delaware, the Battle of Trenton and fights with the Hessians. Lincoln mesmerized the legislature with his folksy humor and humbleness and thanked them for coming out despite not voting for him.[293] In the 1860 election, Lincoln did not carry the state. New Jersey was the only northern state not to give all its electoral votes to him.[294] Still, Lincoln's reverence for the state's history was sincere. He observed that out of all the original thirteen states, New Jersey had the most battlefields related to the Revolution.[295] But Lincoln also warned that in the present situation, bloodshed would only happen if the South forced it. According to historian Eric Foner, "When Lincoln told the Democrat-dominated New Jersey General Assembly that while he cherished peace, 'it may be necessary to put the foot down,' the legislature broke out in wild, prolonged cheering."[296] After his address, Lincoln was a guest at a state dinner at the Trenton House. In all, his welcome to New Jersey was very cordial.[297] But were they really cheering because they agreed with Lincoln, or were they just pretending? Lincoln's remarks on the Revolutionary War may not have been accidental or coincidental.

Interestingly, Governor Olden did not attend Lincoln's state address or reception in Trenton, since he was participating in the Peace Conference. Aside from his apparent agreement with the South, being absent during Lincoln's visit sent a nonverbal signal to New Jersey residents that he was not in line with the Republican Party. Lincoln was the president-elect of his own party, and as a member, Olden should have been present to at least greet him.

ON WASHINGTON'S BIRTHDAY, LINCOLN arrived in Philadelphia and visited Independence Hall, where he raised the flag in a symbolic gesture and promised the Union would be saved.[298] While in Philadelphia, Lincoln felt the need to address a comment he had made in New York City, wrote historian Doris Kearns Goodwin. Inside Independence Hall, Lincoln clarified earlier statements that his beliefs about the Declaration of Independence came from his understanding that not only did the thirteen colonies stand together to oppose their mother country, England, but their founding document, the Declaration, also "provided hope to the world for all future time. It was that which gave promise that in due time the weights

Independence Hall, Philadelphia, Pennsylvania. *Author's photo.*

should be lifted from the shoulders of all men, and that *all* should have an equal chance."[299] Lincoln's action of raising the flag over Independence Hall could be viewed as a recommitment to the principles of freedom for all, and maybe it was his way of pledging to finally fulfill the obligation to all Americans declared eighty-four years earlier in that sacred building. Lincoln may have also been contrasting the Peace Democrats/Convention with the British peace commissioners sent to the United States during the Revolutionary War. Those British commissioners, Frederick Earl of Carlisle, Richard Viscount Howe, Sir William Howe, William Eden and George Johnstone, arrived with letters of compromise from Parliament, but the Continental Congress rejected those advances and instead issued its manifesto, which read in part:

> *We, therefore, the Congress of the United States of America, do solemnly declare and proclaim that if our enemies presume to execute their threats, or persist in their present career of barbarity, we will take such exemplary vengeance as shall deter others from a like conduct. We appeal to that God who searcheth the hearts of men, for the rectitude of our intentions, and*

in his holy presence we declare, that as we are not moved by any light and hasty suggestions of anger or revenge, so through every possible change of fortune we will adhere to this determination.

The portals of the temple we have raised to freedom shall then be thrown wide, as an asylum to mankind. America shall receive to her bosom and comfort and cheer the oppressed, the miserable and the poor of every nation and of every clime.

We shall learn to consider all men as our brethren, being equal children of the Universal Parent—that God of the heavens and of the earth.[300]

In this manifesto, Congress made clear its intention to stand its ground on Independence and doubled down, so to speak, on its plan to make America a country for all people. By hoisting the flag over the site where not only was the Declaration of Independence signed but Congress also refused to compromise to end the Revolutionary War, Lincoln was sending a strong signal that he would correct the course of the United States and not give in to his present-day "peace commissioners" who brought false peace and reconciliation to the nation.

During the antebellum period, White and Black New Jersey residents refused to let anti-Black and proslavery voices go unchallenged. Abolitionists took on those who spread misinformation about their real intentions to further Black equality and citizenship and end slavery by opposing legislative efforts that supported colonization. They also responded by actively rallying the public to their cause. Despite the abolitionists' undertakings, copperhead politicians succeeded in stalling Black rights and convincing some Whites that freedmen in the state or fugitives fleeing cruelty were real threats to White society. At the same time, Peace Democrats also attempted to block the Lincoln administration in any way possible, including by undertaking efforts to foil Lincoln's goal to maintain the Union. Colonization advocates spread misinformation about their plan and portrayed a false dream of Black freedom in Africa. These proponents continually called for Whites to contribute to their cause while actively trying to convince free Blacks that their only option for freedom was to be exiled to a foreign country and continent with no relatives and very little resources. They may have thought they were halting progress for good, but in reality, winds of change were blowing, and civil war would force America to deal with its true cause of greater worth—freedom.

CHAPTER 6

"GOD WON'T LET MASSA LINCOLN BEAT THE SOUTH TILL HE DO THE RIGHT THING"

Lydia Maria Child met Harriet Tubman in January 1862 while working with contraband at Fortress Monroe, Virginia, and was impressed with her courage and knowledge of politics. In a letter to fellow writer John G. Whittier, Child remarked on Tubman's wise pronouncements. "She said the other day: They may send the flower of their young men down South, to die.…All no use! God's ahead of Massa Lincoln. God won't let Massa Lincoln beat the South till he do the right thing.…He do it by setting the negroes free."[301]

SALT PETER

In July 1862, the U.S. Congress enacted the Militia Act, allowing Blacks to work as laborers for the Union army or as soldiers.[302] Earlier, in May 1862, the War Department issued General Order 143, creating the United States Colored Troops (USCT) and officially permitting Black men to enlist in the Union army.[303] The Black men who enlisted, in particular those from New Jersey who joined the Twenty-Second Regiment USCT, became mighty fighting machines. They were the salt peter (or petre) of the Civil War— the essential missing ingredient—needed to win. During the Revolutionary War, the Continental army began running low on ammunition. There were not enough furnaces in the colonies to produce lead shot or gunpowder, so individuals began experimenting to make the needed supplies by melting lead from windows and household ornaments.[304] The innovation came because the usual manner of obtaining the necessary lead was shut off by the British. In order to successfully battle back, the Continental army needed to improvise. This same thinking came into being in the Civil War. A new method of waging war was needed. During the Civil War, African American men were the necessary infusion of black powder to win the war against slavery and the Confederates.

Frederick Douglass, fugitive slave, abolitionist. *Courtesy of Library of Congress.*

Frederick Douglass wrote, "The FIRST of January, 1863, was a memorable day in the progress of American liberty and civilization. It was the turning-point in the conflict between freedom and slavery. A death-blow was given to the slaveholding rebellion."[305] President Lincoln issued the Emancipation Proclamation on January 1, 1863, freeing all slaves held in southern states that seceded. The antislavery movement rejoiced; copperheads and rebels detested the announcement. Nonetheless, the Confederate congress had anticipated such a move and earlier decreed that any Black soldier captured would be sold as a slave or killed.[306] The Confederate government issued a proclamation known as the Black Flag in December 1862 that any captured Blacks in uniform would be taken as slaves and turned over to the state they belonged to for re-enslavement. This was because Confederates viewed all Blacks as slaves and those fighting with the Federals as slaves in revolt. The southern Cavalier code of honor did not allow them to give quarter to captured Blacks. Confederates issued the proclamation after Union general Benjamin Butler began using and arming Blacks in New Orleans. Under the Black Flag, White officers in command of Black troops were also punished and subject to be treated as criminals deserving death or imprisonment. White noncommissioned officers and soldiers captured under the Black Flag were considered prisoners of war (POWs).[307]

The Confederate congress then passed resolutions addressing captured commissioned Federal army officers. Section 1 declared that the Confederate government would control how captives would be disposed.

Section 2 stipulated that proclamations from the U.S. Congress and Lincoln emancipating slaves in Southern states would be viewed as insurrection and retaliated against. Section 3 confirmed that actions against citizens of Southern states would be violations of Confederate law and retaliated against. Section 4 asserted White commissioned officers of Black troops who were captured could possibly be punished by death. Section 5 provided for the same punishment for White noncommissioned officers. Section 6 stated that all persons charged would be tried before a military court. Section 7 declared that all Blacks captured as soldiers or found giving aid to the enemy would be handed over to the state in which they were captured

Union general Benjamin Butler. *Courtesy of Library of Congress.*

to be dealt with by those laws.[308] In March 1863, the Confederate congress passed two more resolutions pertaining just to Blacks: Section 9 asserted that no slave could be impressed for labor by the Confederate government if that labor could be obtained by hiring Blacks and that slaves who were impressed would be under the regulations and laws of the state they worked in, and Section 10 declared that before December 1, 1863, no slave working on a farm or plantation could be taken for public use without their owner's consent, except for emergencies. The Confederate government eventually lifted the section of the Black Flag that would commit Black Union soldiers who were never slaves to slavery.[309]

After Black Union soldiers were captured at Charleston and not exchanged as POWs like their White counterparts, President Lincoln issued an order on July 30, 1863, pledging government support to protect them. Then Lincoln warned the Confederate government that for every captured Black POW killed, enslaved or put to hard labor, the same would be done to one of their POWs.[310]

Threats did not deter New Jersey Black men from enlisting. This cause was the greatest one for African Americans in the nineteenth century. They were no longer going to be denied. After the Emancipation Proclamation was issued, Massachusetts Republican senator Charles Sumner, who was also an abolitionist, delivered the bill calling for enlistment of three hundred thousand Black troops. His home state then organized the Black regiments

Fifty-Fourth and Fifty-Fifth Massachusetts. Many Black Philadelphians and men from New Jersey traveled to Massachusetts to join those regiments.[311] Black men from the Delaware Valley, like Robert George Fitzgerald, rushed to join regiments in New York City and Massachusetts. Fitzgerald first signed up as a seaman in New York City, but after a year's service, he decided to switch to the Fifth Cavalry training in Readville, Massachusetts. According to historian Cheryl Renée Gooch, Fitzgerald wrote in his diary that he and his comrades joined the service after hearing Frederick Douglass speak on enlistment. He contended they all wanted "to go to the front where we can prove our love of Liberty and that we be men."[312] Other Black veterans admitted after the war that they enlisted to fight for freedom for their people and that saving the Union came second.[313] Frank H. Taylor, a contemporary of the times, wrote, "So deeply rooted was the old prejudice in Philadelphia against the Blacks, that recruits raised here for the two above designated regiments were sent away at night in small squads by rail."[314]

On July 6, 1863, Frederick Douglass spoke in Philadelphia urging Black men to enlist, stating in part:

> *The hour has arrived, and your place is in the Union army. Remember that the musket, the United States musket with its bayonet of steel, is better than all mere parchment guarantees liberty. In your hands that musket means liberty; and should your constitutional rights at the close of the war be denied, which, in the nature of things, it cannot be, your brethren are safe while you have a Constitution which proclaims your right to keep and bear arms.[315]*

Prominent White Philadelphians—such as F.C. Philpot, James Logan, J. Miller McKim, William Rotch Wister and Cadwalader Biddle, to name a few—met in March and June 1863 to discuss raising Black regiments in the city and countering that prejudicial spirit. Then on June 1, 1863, Lieutenant Colonel Charles C. Ruff told the Citizens' Bounty Fund Committee that he was ordered to create one regiment of ten companies of colored troops, with eighty men in each company, to be used in service to the United States. The next week, Camp William Penn was established as the site for training Black troops. The camp was located outside the city limits in Cheltenham Township, Montgomery County, Pennsylvania.[316] Initially, the camp was to be built on land owned by Jay Cooke, an abolitionist and financier of the war, but it was moved to another location on land donated by Edward Davis.[317] Quaker abolitionist Lucretia Mott and her husband, James, moved from Philadelphia to a farmhouse and residence on Davis's property in the

Camp William Penn, Cheltenham Township, Pennsylvania. *Courtesy of Library of Congress.*

late 1850s. Edward Davis was the Motts' son-in-law. There, Lucretia Mott assisted fugitives along the UGRR, and once the camp was in operation, the Motts helped the soldiers who were in training there.[318]

Once the government adopted the policy of organizing colored troops, a free military school was established in Philadelphia to train White officers for those regiments. The requirements were necessarily strict: candidates needed to be physically fit and competent in understanding military regulations for officers and possess the temperament to train and address former slaves and freedmen who might be illiterate and unaccustomed to contact with Whites. One requirement in the pamphlet *Free Military School for Applicants for Commands of Colored Troops* stated: "Military Knowledge must precede talent, zeal, sympathy for negro troops and it must also be in unison with the power to command men in battle."[319] The board of examiners wanted the best candidates, and as a result, about 47 percent of White applicants were rejected for leadership positions.[320] Only men of good character were selected for the school. Each candidate had to apply by writing a letter requesting admission. Those that qualified were allowed to study and take the exam. Once the White candidates passed a physical and the preliminary exams, the preceptor recommended the best candidates for appearance before the board. "I hope you will stand as a high wall to keep out all drones, all nincompoops, all mere snivelers, and send us your good, wide-awake, clean headed young men of the true ring—the best material offered for line officers is of the noncommissioned officers in the army—they as a class are superior to the commissioned officers of the army," according to the board's preceptor. While they waited, those candidates were permitted to go to Camp William Penn to temporarily practice the functions of an officer.[321]

The outline for how to organize Black regiments and officers was established by Union major general David Hunter in May 1862, when he took command of Black troops in the South Carolina Volunteer Regiment. Hunter only accepted qualified candidates for command of his Black troops, and they needed more than the regular understanding of military tactics and procedures. These White officers needed character, courage and a true desire to train Black men into soldiers.[322] In May 1863, President Lincoln decided to disregard the practice begun by some generals of assigning unqualified White men to be officers over the Black troops. He also appointed a board to review White men applying for commands in colored regiments. Wilson wrote that by 1863, White men viewed the command of a Black regiment as an achievement. He argued that it was "a coveted prize, for which men of wealth and education contended."[323] Having properly trained and fit officers of good moral character who had a heart for instructing Black men was of value to the army, since improperly trained Black soldiers would reflect poorly on the military. But it was also necessary for the morale of Black soldiers to know that they received the knowledge and preparation needed to successfully wage war and save their own lives and those of their comrades. In addition, being properly trained would show the nation that they possessed the manliness to be called soldiers, men and citizens.

Once the war started, concerned Philadelphia men loyal to the Union began meeting to discuss how to support the Lincoln administration. The group of leading men adopted the title Union League for their organization, and by February 23, 1863, their membership totaled 536 "and the Union League became at once a potent center of aggressive Union effort," wrote Taylor.[324] As soon as Camp William Penn was organized, the Union League began promoting assistance, spending $33,000 on equipment and other things for the troops and presenting each regiment with a "stand of colors." In 1865, the Union League moved into its building on Broad Street in Philadelphia.[325] One week after the camp was established, its first commander, Lieutenant Colonel Louis Wagner, was appointed.[326] Born in Germany, Wagner joined the Eighty-Eighth Pennsylvania Infantry Regiment and was injured during the Second Battle of Bull Run,[327] fought in Northern

Union League Club, Philadelphia, Pennsylvania. *Author's photo.*

Virginia from July 14 through August 27, 1862.[328] Wagner also fought in the battles of Cedar Mountain (August 9, 1862), Groveton and Thoroughfare Gap (August 28–30, 1862) and Rappahannock Station (November 7, 1863).[329] Wagner strongly supported the Black troops under his command and complained about the mistreatment of Black soldiers in Philadelphia.[330] A seasoned soldier, Wagner brought not only battle experience to his position but also compassion.

A few months following Wagner's appointment, Joseph Barr Kiddoo was promoted to colonel of the 22nd Regiment USCT on January 6, 1864. Kiddoo was a battle-hardened soldier who understood what was required of good soldiers and the hardships ahead for these men. He enlisted in the Union army in April 1862, joining the 12th Pennsylvania. After his discharge in August, he enlisted with the 63rd Pennsylvania, serving in battles at Yorktown and Williamsburg (April 5–May 4, 1862), and Fair Oaks and Malvern Hill (July 1, 1862). He was later commissioned as lieutenant colonel of the 137th Pennsylvania and then promoted to colonel on March 15, 1863. Kiddoo fought at South Mountain (September 14, 1862), Antietam (September 17, 1862), Fredericksburg (December 13, 1862) and Chancellorsville (April

26–May 6, 1863). On June 1, 1863, Kiddoo mustered out, then reenlisted on October 5, 1863, becoming a major in the 6th U.S. Colored Infantry. He was then promoted to colonel of the 22nd Regiment USCT. Kiddoo was injured in the Petersburg assault while serving as colonel of the 22nd Regiment and was brevetted for that action. He retired after the war, in 1870, with the rank of brigadier general USV.[331]

As with the selection of Wagner, the army assigned to a Black regiment another White officer, Kiddoo, who had battle experience, military knowledge and also a commitment to the men he was about to lead. Kiddoo was the right man for Black men from South Jersey, an area where resistance to slavery and inequality were almost inbred. He was

Union colonel Joseph Barr Kiddoo, Twenty-Second Regiment USCT. *Courtesy of Library of Congress.*

also the right colonel to lead Black South Jersey soldiers in the Twenty-Second Regiment USCT, having been in some of the bloodiest battles of the Civil War, including Antietam, the bloodiest one-day battle of the war, waged near Antietam Creek outside Sharpsburg, Maryland. Federal and Confederate troops fought in continuous back-and-forth maneuvers, with the focal point of the most intense fighting around a sunken road, where Federal troops, positioned on elevated land, engulfed Confederates on the lower ground with withering gunfire. The slaughter was so intense that the sunken road became known as Bloody Lane.[332] When the battle ended, Federal forces had lost 12,401 in dead and wounded and the Confederates 10,318. The Confederate defeat was a one-two punch to their cause. It dampened potential foreign support and recognition from Europe and gave Lincoln a win so that he could issue the Emancipation Proclamation.[333] Fredericksburg was the site of a Federal assault that should have succeeded but failed due to missteps and missed opportunities on the Union side. This time, Federal forces were gunned down on a sunken road by Confederates situated behind an elevated stone wall after repeatedly committing soldiers to a frontal assault on enemy lines. The final cost: Union forces lost 13,000 men, and the Confederates lost only 5,000. But the rebel win gave them the confidence to attack the North at Gettysburg the following summer in July 1863 and prevented the Federals from reaching Richmond.[334] Having participated in such fierce battles, Kiddoo was well prepared to lead fighting men like those of the Twenty-Second Regiment USCT.

To encourage Black enlistment, the city issued a recruitment circular that was signed by sixty-four prominent African American leaders and men such as Frederick Douglass, William D. Forten, William Whipper, Reverend Stephen Smith, O.V. Catto, Reverend William T. Catto and David B. Bowser.[335] The circular was a call to arms for the African American community. It encouraged Black men to take charge of the moment, reading in part:

> *This is our golden moment. The Government of the United States calls for every able-bodied colored man to enter the army for the three years' service, and join in fighting the battles of Liberty and the Union. A new era is open to us. For generations we have suffered under the horrors of slavery outrage and wrong! Our manhood has been denied, our citizenship blotted out, our souls seared and burned, our spirits cowed and crushed, and the hopes of the future of our race involved in doubt and darkness. If we love our country, if we love our families, our children, our homes, we must strike now while the country calls. More than a million of white men have left comfortable homes and joined the armies of the Union to save their country. Cannot we leave ours and swell the hosts of the Union, save our liberties, vindicate our manhood and deserve well of our country?[336]*

Camp William Penn mustered eleven colored regiments between 1863 and 1865: the 3rd, 6th, 8th, 22nd, 24th, 25th, 32nd, 41st, 43rd, 45th and 127th.[337] Many Black men from New Jersey flocked to Cheltenham Township to join one of the regiments. This was the opportunity John Rock dreamed about. He wrote:

> *Sooner or later, the clashing of arms will be heard in this country, and the black man's service will be needed: 150,000 freemen capable of bearing arms, and not all cowards and fools, and three quarters of a million slaves, wild with the enthusiasm caused by the dawn of the glorious opportunity of being able to strike a genuine blow for freedom, will be a power, which white men will be "bound to respect."[338]*

Rock ended his statement with a paraphrase of the infamous Dred Scott decision handed down by U.S. Supreme Court chief justice Roger Brooke Taney, who wrote that Blacks had "no rights which the white man was bound to respect."[339] The Dred Scott case (*Scott v. Sandford)* was decided in 1857 and involved a slave named Dred Scott whose master took him to live in the free state of Illinois. Later, they moved to the northern section of the Louisiana Purchase, territory where slavery was not permitted under the Missouri Compromise. When he returned to the state of Missouri, Scott sued for freedom, citing the fact he had lived in a free state, which made him free. But the majority of the Supreme Court held that he was not a citizen and could not bring suit in court. Taney spoke for the high court, stating that since the Missouri Compromise was unconstitutional, masters could take their property anywhere in the territories and retain their legal title to it.[340] Abolitionists in the North decried this decision, asserting Blacks were indeed citizens in some states.[341]

As hundreds of Black men from New Jersey flocked to Camp William Penn, the state lost the chance to have those recruits credited to its numbers because Governor Joel Parker (Democrat, 1863–66 and 1872–75) failed to encourage Black recruitment and local municipalities delayed claiming credit for Black residents who joined USCT regiments.[342] Parker was a states' rights copperhead who defended slavery, disparaged Blacks and railed against the Lincoln administration. In an 1864 speech, Parker addressed emancipation and the war, alleging that the condition of the country was "truly deplorable" because of the war, which had increased the national debt to limits that "[have]" reduced to comparative poverty many who supposed they had a competency" and would hurt future generations.[343] He contended that Lincoln subjugated the Constitution, suppressed free speech and the press and "undermined" trial by jury and habeas corpus, essentially violating states' rights.[344] Parker also called Lincoln a "usurper" and blamed abolitionists for destroying the federal compact and turning slavery into a sin. "It is a State institution…the right to regulate which was never yielded by the States," he argued."[345]

The governor was not the only one to dislike the idea of Black troops fighting the war. So did many White New Jerseyans.[346] Yet there were Whites who praised the effort to allow Blacks to fight in the military. A writer to the *Continental Monthly*, Henry Everett Russell, recalled seeing colored troops as a child. Now, in 1864, he believed Black enlistment would elevate the race:

> *Thus the employment of the negro as a soldier, while it must inspire the bondsmen of the South with a truer sense of his worth and capacity, and thus tend to weaken the foundation of the whole rebel fabric, will also correct the unquestioned evil of a growing class of outlaws in the midst of*

our society. And if we clothe the negro in the uniform of a soldier of the United States, the respect of the nation for its brave defenders will teach him self-respect; at the same time that it will teach the nation to put a new value upon its idea of loyalty.[347]

No matter how much Democrats hated the idea of Black troops fighting in the war, they were coming, and Camp William Penn was churning them out battle-ready. Douglass spoke at the camp in a recruitment promotion on July 24, 1863, to encourage the men on their upcoming missions. Later in 1863, both he and Harriet Tubman spoke to the Black regiments that were about to go to war.[348] Tubman was a frequent visitor to the camp, offering words of encouragement, confidence and pride in the troops. In April 1865, she addressed the Twenty-Fourth Regiment USCT at Camp William Penn. Tubman also went to the camp to see her old friend Lucretia Mott, with whom she had connections as an UGRR conductor, having brought many fugitives to the Mott home and other stations in the area.[349]

As Black men rushed to enlist at Camp William Penn, one regiment, the Twenty-Second, became the most heavily joined by men from New Jersey and particularly South Jersey. It was called the "most 'Jersey' of all USCT regiments, with 681 Jersey men on its rolls."[350] At least 992 African Americans from Gloucester, Camden, Cumberland and Salem Counties volunteered in the various regiments at the camp.[351] Approximately 16 African American men are listed on the roll of residents from Franklin Township, Gloucester County, who served in the Civil War, although many of these names were not listed on the 1860 U.S. Census for the township.[352] It is possible that many of these men became township residents during the war or following the conflict. Among those 681 Jersey men who were selected to be part of the Twenty-Second Regiment USCT were John W. Hicks and William Tribbitt (spelled "Tribit" on some documents); both volunteered for Franklin Township, Gloucester County, New Jersey.[353]

Hicks was thirty-four years old in 1864 when he enlisted. He was assigned to Company E, Twenty-Second Regiment.[354] The U.S. Census for 1860 showed Hicks living in Franklin Township, working as a laborer and living with his twenty-five-year-old wife Sarah A. Hicks and their two children, six-year-old Angelina and two-year-old John W. The census also showed that both Hicks and his wife were from Delaware. If that is true, most likely they left that state because of slavery. They had been living in New Jersey for at least six years, since the census showed that Angelina and John Jr. were born in the Garden State. Although neither parent could read or write, their daughter could, which was an indication she was enrolled in school.[355] Interestingly, on his enlistment record, Hicks stated he was born in Maryland. Could he have been a fugitive slave? Did he misidentify where he was from on the 1860 census because he was afraid of being found by his owner? Was he emancipated? Or was he afraid of being targeted by state officials who wanted to remove Blacks who moved into New Jersey from other states, believing they were fugitives? If Hicks was a fugitive, that would have been cause enough to join the Union army.

1860 U.S. Census: Black Families and Singles Living in Franklin Township, Gloucester County

Andrew Thomas: Age 35, male, Black, laborer, value of estate $11, born in North NJ
  Martha Thomas: Age 28, female, Black, born in North NJ
  Andrew Thomas: Age 2, male, Black
  Martha Thomas: Age 2½ months, female, Black

Jacob Maxland: Age 32, male, Black, value of estate $10, laborer
  Nancy: Age 20, female, Black
  Victoria: 7½ months, female, Black

Abram Harris: Age 60, male, Black, laborer, value of real estate $50, value of personal estate $20, born in NJ, could not read or write
  Sarah Purance: Age 40, female, Black, born in NJ
  Ashton Harris: Age 12, male, Black, born in NJ
  Elizabeth: Age 10, female, Black, born in NJ
  Louisa C.: Age 8, female, Black, born in NJ
  Emelina Ashton: Age 6, female, Black, born in NJ
  Ebenezer Ashton: Age 4, male, Black, born in NJ
  Isabella Ashton: Age 1, female, Black, born in NJ

Joseph Spencer: Age 70, male, Black, value of personal estate $10, laborer, born in PA, could read and write
  Louisa Spencer: Age 40, female, Black, born in PA, could read and write
  Mary J. Spencer: Age 8, female, Black, born in north NJ, could read and write
  Thomas Spencer: Age 15, male, Black, born in PA, could read and write
  Emma White: Age 28, female, Black, born in PA, could read and write

HENRY JOHNSON: Age 45, male, Black, value of personal estate $10, laborer, born in PA, could read and write
   Lydia Johnson: Age 40, female, born in PA, could read and write
   Hester Johnson: Age 17, female, Black, born in PA, could read and write
   William Johnson: Age 13, male, Black, born in PA, could read and write

ABSALOM MUSTANG: Age 40, male, Black, laborer, could not read and write

JOHN WILLIAMS: Age 27, male, Black, value of personal property $10, born in PA, laborer, could read and write
   Rachel Williams: Age 25, female, Black, born in PA, could read and write
   Catharine Williams: Age 4, female, Black, born in PA
   Andrew Jackson: Age 30, male, Black, born in PA, could read and write
   Mary Jackson: Age 40, female, Black, born in PA, could read and write
   Hannah Chase: Age 18, female, Black, born in PA, could read and write
   John Chase: Age 14, male, Black, born in PA, could read and write
   Ellen J. Chase: Age 11, female, Black, born in PA, could read and write
   Louisa Chase: Age 7, female, Black, born in PA, could read and write
   John W. Jackson: Age 14, male, Black, born in PA, could read and write
   Lewis E. Jackson: Age 1, male, Black, born in PA

ISAAC RILEY: Age 65, male, Black, value of real estate $200, value of personal property $20, laborer, born in DE, could not read or write
   Ann Riley: Age 45, female, Black, born in DE, could not read or write
   Isaac Riley: Age 8, male, Black, born in NJ, could read and write
   John H. Riley: Age 12, male, Black, born in NJ, could read and write
   Elizabeth Riley: Age 18, female, Black, born in NJ, could read and write

JOHN W. HICKS: Age 28, male, Black, laborer, born in DE, could not read or write
   Sarah A. Hicks: Age 25, female, Black, born in DE, could not read or write
   Angelina Hicks: Age 6, female, Black, born in NJ, could read and write
   John W. Hicks: Age 2, male, Black, born in NJ

EDWARD KNIGHT: Age 40, male, Black, value of personal property $20, collier (coal miner), born in Maryland, could not read or write
   Mary A. Knight: Age 40, female, Black, born in NJ, could not read or write
   Thomas D. Knight: Age 25, male, Black

ANDREW JACKSON: Age 40, male, Black, value of personal property $10, laborer, born in DE, could read and write
  Mary A. Jackson: Age 35, female, Black, born in DE, could read and write
  Andrew Jackson: Age 13, male, Black, born in NJ, could read and write
  Mary Chase: Age 11, female, Black, born in NJ, could read and write
  Sophia Chase: Age 9, female, Black, born in NJ, could read and write
  John Chase: Age 1, male, Black, born in NJ

BENJAMIN CLARK: Age 65, male, Black, value of personal property $10, laborer, born in PA.

JOSEPH DUFFARDER: Age 50, male, Black, could not read or write, living with White family: Jos. McKeag and wife Dorothy McKeag, both age 35, White, born in Ireland, husband was a laborer, had property valued at $20; neither could read or write

JOSEPH HOWARD: Age 70, male, Black, listed under Adam Saxer, age 50, male, White, born in Germany

JOSEPH HOWARD: Age 25, male, Black, laborer
  Mary Howard: Age 20, female, Black
  Nathan Howard: Age 1/12 months, male, Black
  All lived with Peter Matlack, age 45, male, White, laborer, value of
    real estate property $1,200, value of personal property $200, born in
    Ireland

JOSEPH W. WINTERBACK: Age 14, male, Black, lived with Lawrence Cake, age 61, male, White, farmer, value of real estate $25,000, value of personal estate $500

SCHEDULE OF ALL BLACK RESIDENTS OF FRANKLIN TOWNSHIP, GLOUCESTER COUNTY, NEW JERSEY: 1860

Total number of Black people: 61
Total number of Black families: 11
Total number of Black men (single and married): 17
Total number of single Black men: 4

Total number of youths over 10 years old living with White people: 1
Total number of Black families living with White people: 1
Total number of single Black men living with White people: 3
Total number of adult Black men aged 25 and up: 17
Total number of Black children under 20 years old: 18
Total number of Black men with real or personal estates: 10

According to research by William H. Skinner on Black Civil War soldiers, Tribbitt may have been recruited for Franklin Township but resided in Winslow Township, Camden County.[356] In 1864, Tribbitt was thirty-one years old.[357] He was one of nine free Black males living in Winslow Township, which was rural in 1860, just like Franklin Township. The total free Black population in Winslow Township was 19 people out of a total population of 1,800, White and Black.[358] The 1860 census for Camden County showed the county had a total free Black population of 2,574 people, the most out of all South Jersey counties, with the city of Camden possessing the largest share of the Black population.[359] On January 5, 1864, Tribbitt enlisted at Camp William Penn and was assigned to Company J, Twenty-Second Regiment.[360] Although he volunteered with the expectation he would serve the country and fight slavery, his experience was not that of Hicks. While in training at camp, Tribbitt was seriously injured. His military record shows he sustained injuries to his spinal cord and bladder in a fall, which also affected his ability to walk.[361] While his comrades continued training at Camp William Penn, Tribbitt was in the camp's hospital trying to recover from his injuries. When his comrades completed training and began their journey south, Tribbitt was still being evaluated. After several months of being incapacitated, medical officials declared him unfit for duty and army officials signed his disability discharge papers.[362] He was officially discharged from the army with an honorable disability discharge on July 22, 1864, after being absent from his regiment from February through July.[363] On his army disability discharge certificate, Tribbitt listed his home as being in Franklin Township.[364] His ordeal highlights how rigorous the training was and how danger was not just on the battlefield. Despite not being able to continue on with his comrades, Tribbitt and many others in his condition still gave all for the cause of freedom.

Military records: *This page, top*: Tribbitt's army medical description. *This page, bottom*: Tribbitt's medical discharge approval. *Opposite, top*: Reverse side of Tribbitt's medical discharge papers. *Opposite, bottom left*: Tribbitt's official army discharge/disability. *Opposite, bottom right*: Tribbitt's muster-out company descriptive book. *National Archives.*

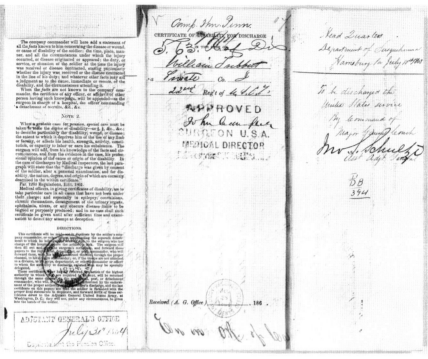

Franklin Township was incorporated in 1820 and consisted of 72,000 acres over 56.42 square miles. The land was flat, with soil that was perfect for cultivation. As a result, much of the township was rural and mainly agricultural, but some sections, like Malaga, Janvier and Clayton, also contained glasshouses, gristmills and sawmills.[365] Gloucester County had many areas that contained marl, a naturally occurring fertilizer composed of clay, calcium and magnesium.[366] This made the soil very rich and perfect for growing crops. Throughout the county and township, there were many farms. The 1860 census showed eleven Black families lived in the township, and there was a total of seventeen single and married Black men aged twenty-five and up.

TABLES & GRAPHS FROM 1860 CENSUS: FRANKLIN TOWNSHIP/ GLOUCESTER COUNTY

Where Blacks in Franklin Township Were Born

New Jersey
Men: 2
Women: 3
Children:
0–12 months old: 3
1–3 years old: 4
4–6 years old: 3
7–10 years old: 5
11–13 years old: 4
14–19 years old: 0

Pennsylvania
Men: 5
Women: 6
Children:
0–12 months old: 0
1–3 years old: 1
4–6 years old: 1
7–10 years old: 1
11–13 years old: 2
14–19 years old: 4

Unknown
Men: 6
Women: 2
Children:
0–12 months: 0
1–3 years old: 0
2–6 years old: 0
7–10 years old: 0
11–13 years old: 0
14–19 years old: 1

Delaware
Men: 3
Women: 4
Children:
0–12 months old: 0
1–3 years old: 0
4–6 years old: 0
7–10 years old: 0
11–13 years old: 0
14–19 years old: 0

Maryland
Men: 1
Women: 0
Children: 0 (all ages)

1860 CENSUS: POPULATION GLOUCESTER COUNTY, NEW JERSEY

Total White population (all ages and genders): 17,737
Total free Black population (all ages and genders): 707
Total White males: 9,152
Total White females: 8,585
Total free Black males: 317
Total free Black females: 310
Total mulatto males: 35
Total mulatto females: 45
Total Black and mulatto (free colored) residents: 707

Aggregate total of White and Black people: 18,444
Total foreign-born (immigrants) residents (these numbers are included in the total White population figures):
White males: 854
White females: 617
(There are no Black foreign-born residents.)

According to that year's census, Gloucester County had a total free Black population of 707 people and no slaves. In that census, the state reported a total free Black population of 25,318 people and 18 un-free apprentices for life (virtual slaves).[367] No slaves were reported in any of the South Jersey counties.

BREAKDOWN BY OCCUPATION: BLACK ADULT MALE RESIDENTS OF FRANKLIN TOWNSHIP, 1860 CENSUS

Benjamin Clark: Laborer
Abram Harris: Laborer
John W. Hicks: Laborer
Joseph Howard: Laborer
Andrew Jackson: Laborer
Henry Johnson: Laborer
Edward Knight: Collier (coal miner)

Jacob Maxland: Laborer
Absalom Mustang: Laborer
Isaac Riley: Laborer
Joseph Spencer: Laborer
Andrew Thomas: Laborer
John Williams: Laborer

No occupation listed on census:
Joseph Duffarder
Joseph Howard (age 70)

MANTUA TOWNSHIP: SINGLE BLACK YOUTHS LIVING WITH
WHITES FROM 1860 U.S. CENSUS REPORTS

HARRIS BLACK: Age 15, female, Black
SARAH THOMAS: Age 10, female, Black
Both listed under Chat. R. White, age 46, male, White, mason, value of
personal estate $100

ANNA M. HARMON: Age 17, female, Black, domestic
Listed under Louisa Rosensodd, age 31, female, White, professional lady,
value of personal estate $500, born in France

JOSEPH REED: Age 10, male, Black, born in PA
Listed under Lewis Aubray, age 53, male, White, gardener, value of real
estate $3,000, value of personal estate $500, born in France

ELIZA RUSSEL: Age 16, female, Black
Listed under Abel Clemens, age 26, male, White, mechanic, value of
personal estate $3,000

PHILIP SHORTER: Age 15, male, Black, laborer
ADELINE SHORTER: Age 18, female, Black, domestic
JENKINS SHORTER: Age 22, male, Black, laborer
All listed under Albert Lippincott, age 24, male, White, farmer, value of
real estate $12,000, value of personal estate $2,000

Mantua Township: Black/Colored Residents, 1860

RICHARD THOMAS: Age 55, male, Black, farmer, value of real estate
$1,500, value of personal estate $100, born in DE
   Anna Thomas: Age 71, female, Black, born in DE

JOHN C. HUGG: Age 46, male, mulatto, farmer, value of personal estate $250, born in NJ

  Mary Hugg: Age 44, female, mulatto, born in NJ
  Bulah Hugg: Age 23, female, mulatto, born in NJ
  Geo. Hugg: Age 21, male, mulatto, born in NJ
  Louisa Hugg: Age 20, female, mulatto, born in NJ
  Priscilla Hugg: Age 17, female, mulatto, born in NJ
  Mary Elizabeth Hugg: Age 16, female, mulatto, born in NJ
  Rebecca Hugg: Age 12, female, mulatto, born in NJ
  Martha Hugg: Age 8, female, mulatto, born in NJ
  John C. Hugg: Age 6½ months, male, mulatto, born in NJ

HARRISON TOWNSHIP: SINGLE BLACK YOUTHS LIVING WITH WHITES, 1860 CENSUS

JANE DENT: Age 17, female, Black, domestic
Listed under Jesse Lippincott, age 41, male, White, farmer, value of real estate $25,000, value of personal estate $11,000

ALLEN DAVID: Age 9, male, Black
Listed under Wm. Dyer, age 31, male, White, farmer

CAMELIA COOPER: Age 15, female, Black, domestic
Listed under Horock Mulford, age 26, male, White, landlord, value of real estate $4,000, value of personal estate $500, born in NJ

CHARLES CLEAVER: Age 14, male, Black, born in NJ
Listed under Jeremiah Chapman, age 57, male, White, farmer, value of real estate $8,000, value of personal estate $4,000, born in NJ

MALINA BORKIN: Age 11, female, Black, born in PA
Listed under Geo. Beehes, age 44, male, White, farmer, value of real estate $20,000, value of personal estate $4,000, born in NJ

ISAIAH BELL: Age 12, male, Black
Listed under Geo. T. Atkinson, age 49, male, White, farmer, value of real estate $15,000, value of personal estate $2,000

Black Families Living in Harrison Township, 1860

JONATHAN FINNAMAN: Age 69, male, Black, laborer, value of personal estate $150, born in PA
  Emmeline Finnaman: Age 59, female, Black, born in PA, cannot read or write
  John H. Waples: Age 30, male, Black, born in DE, married within the year
  Anna Waples: Age 16, female, Black, born in NJ, married within the year

Although Franklin Township was rural in the early to mid-1800s, there was one landmark that the people from the area would have been familiar with seeing and that still exists today: the Franklinville Inn, a stagecoach stop tavern/inn that began operating in the colonial era. The inn is located at the far end of the township on what is now known as Delsea Drive. This road was a main stagecoach route to the county seat, Woodbury, and the Delaware River going northwestward and to Cape May going southeastward. The men would have passed this landmark on their way to Camp William Penn. Maybe Hicks or Tribbitt even enjoyed a beer or other drink there as residents before enlisting.

Historic Franklinville Inn, colonial-era stagecoach stop, Franklinville. *Author's photo.*

When it was time for the volunteers to go to camp, they said goodbye to their families and traveled to Camden to board a ferry to Philadelphia. Once in the city, they may have been let off at the Washington Street Pier, then either walked or took a carriage to the Pennsylvania Railroad depot in the city center. There the men boarded a horse-drawn streetcar with an open platform behind the passenger cabins to ride to the camp. The Black men most likely were not allowed to ride inside the segregated cars.[368] At camp, the Black soldiers were subject to a stringent and regulated routine. According to historian James Paradis, a typical day was:

Reveille & Roll Call	*6 AM*
Surgeon's Call	*6:30 AM*
Breakfast	*7 AM*
Sergeant's Call	*7:30 AM*
(For morning report)	
Drill	*8 AM*
Adjutants	*9 AM*
Guard Mounting	*10:30 AM*
Sergeant's Call	*11 AM*
(To get morning reports)	
Dinner	*12 noon*
Drill Battalion Call	*3 PM*
Dress Parade	*5:30 PM*
Supper	*6 PM*
Tattoo & Roll	*8:30 PM*
Taps	*9 PM*

On Saturdays, the troops had no battalion drill, but companies still formed at one thirty in the afternoon to clean the camp. Inspections were done at eight thirty in the morning, and on Sundays, they had to attend church services at four o'clock.[369]

Black troops at camp received the same quality of uniforms and arms as White troops. Author Joseph G. Bilby wrote that men in the Twenty-Second Regiment were issued Springfield muzzle-loading rifle muskets. These rifles were standard issue, firing .58-caliber "mini balls," conical hollow lead projectiles. Powder wrapped in a paper cartridge was used for a charge to fire the balls. Soldiers had to tear the cartridge open with their teeth, pour it down the gun barrel, throw away the paper, ram the bullet down and then cap the "cone under the hammer with a copper percussion cap containing an explosive compound."[370] Recruits were paid a bounty of thirty-three dollars when they were mustered in but had the cost of their clothing deducted from their pay. The muster roll of Private James Still from Burlington County showed he was twenty-nine years old when he was enlisted by Captain and Provost Marshall J.B. Coppuck on January 16, 1865, in Trenton. His enlistment was credited to Southampton Township, Burlington County, Second District as a New Jersey recruit. Still was furnished with a knapsack and straps, haversack, canteen and straps, tin cup, plate, spoon, knife and fork. The value of these items was included in his clothing account.[371] The uniform of the Black troops was different from White troops'. Wilson stated that Black infantry troops were dressed in a blue-black dress coat, while the artillery and cavalry wore dark blue jackets. All the uniforms were trimmed with brass buttons and white, red and yellow cord, representing the arm of their service. The men wore heavy sky-blue pants and flannel caps or "a high crown black felt hat with a black feather looped upon the right side and fastened with a brass eagle. For the infantry and the cavalry two swords crossed; for the artillery two cannons on the front of the *chapeau* [hat] crossed, with the letters of the company, and number of the regiment to which the soldier belonged."[372]

Black men at camp trained hard but were able to relax during their free time. Captain Thomas Wentworth Higginson recorded his views of Black soldiers when he served as an officer of Black troops in the First Carolina Regiment in 1862. Before joining the army, Higginson was an ordained Unitarian minister and abolitionist who became involved in John Brown's "Secret Six" cabal. He was also involved in Boston's antislavery movement and the UGRR. As commander of the First Carolina, made up of former slaves who were uneducated, he noted the men had few vices, were mild-mannered, learned quickly and were affectionate toward one another and talkative when not on duty. Higginson wrote, "In all respects they seem better material for soldiers than I had dared to hope for."[373] Higginson pondered how Whites could not see the wit, cunning or intelligence Black people possessed. He also noticed how the pride of those Black men rose, being in the army. When his troops marched into battle, he commented it made him proud to see them in uniform with rifles, "a regiment of freed slaves marching on into the future,—it was something to remember."[374]

There had to be something special about the Black New Jerseyans at Camp William Penn that the White officers saw and made them determined to select them for the Twenty-Second Regiment USCT. Was it a warrior quality? Or potential—a pugnacious tenacity tempered with sobriety—that *something* that cannot be taught, but only improved on? At camp, they must have shined. Now, they were about to burn in Virginia. Once the Twenty-Second Regiment USCT completed training at Camp William Penn, the soldiers were ordered to Virginia. Under the command of Colonel Kiddoo, the Twenty-Second Regiment took the train to the North Philadelphia Railroad Station, got off and marched with the U.S. and their regimental flags flittering in the wind, raised high by color-bearers like Sergeant Edward Richardson from Salem County, who was a former slave from Cecil County, Maryland. After settling in New Jersey, he joined the army and was selected for Company A, Twenty-Second Regiment.[375] The regimental flag was designed by Black painter David Bustill Bowser.[376] It depicted a Black soldier from the Twenty-Second Regiment standing over a fallen Confederate officer, who is about to swing his sword just as the Black soldier bayonets him. Lying on the ground next to the fallen rebel is his flag, a felonious emblem of hate and injustice, now in a state of defeat in the dirt. Above the image is the Latin phrase "*Sic semper tyrannis*" (thus so always to tyrants), inscribed on a ribbon on the front side, and below the image is a ribbon with "22nd Reg: U.S. Colored Troops."

Members of the Twenty-Second Regiment from South Jersey, such as Hicks, Richardson, Still and Andrew Jackson of Company I, would have

Twenty-Second USCT Regimental Flag, front (*left*) and back (*right*). *Author's photo.*

marched through Philadelphia streets to the waterfront dock at Washington Street on the Delaware River to catch the transport south—to enemy territory.[377] As the steamer prepared to shove off from the Philadelphia pier, the South Jersey soldiers of the Twenty-Second Regiment took their place, probably full of anticipation, but their expectations were not greater than those of their family members and friends, who now had their own joining the fight. Streams of tears of joy most likely flowed from the faces of loved ones as they waved their goodbyes as the transports moved away from the wharf and made their way down the Delaware River. Yet these soldiers were carrying more than the hopes and dreams of their families and friends. They were shouldering the burdens and prayers of a people—all of the fugitives' yearnings and freedmen's reckoning.

Before shoving off from the City of Brotherly Love, they would have seen Cooper's Ferry Landing across the river in Camden, where approximately seventy-eight years earlier, shackled and enslaved men, women and children were brought off ships to be sold before the state prohibited slave importations.[378] Modern-day residents will find at the location of the former slave market the Cooper Public Library, built in the early twentieth century. A few blocks downriver from Cooper's Ferry, they may have seen Macedonia AME Church standing tall a block from the riverfront, where congregants rescued a captured fugitive from slave catchers outside the church. In the same area, they would have seen the Black community of Fettersville, started by a Quaker to give Black workers a chance at homeownership. As they steamed a little farther downriver, they passed many inlets and minor waterways, such as Raccoon Creek, which flows through Swedesboro, where fugitives on the UGRR sought shelter and continued on with their suspenseful journey,

View of center city Philadelphia from the Camden side of the Delaware River. *Author's photo.*

and where some of them may have heard about the all-night shootout at Johnson's Tavern between slave catchers and Black community members attempting to rescue a captured fugitive. As the steamer rounded the bend near Pennsville, they would have seen Salem Cove, which flows past Salem city, where a brave slave mother escaped from an armed slave catcher through a courthouse window, or where a slave named Amy Reckless freed herself and then began working on the UGRR, or where abolitionist Abigail Goodwin hid, fed, clothed and spirited off scores of fugitive slaves and Black dentist (and future doctor and lawyer) John Rock trained. As they entered Delaware Bay, they steamed past the expansive and formidable Mad Horse Creek and marsh, which many escaped slaves traversed to reach safety. A little farther down the bay, they saw Stow Creek flowing as a border between Salem and Cumberland Counties. At its entrance to the bay, they would have seen shanties established by Black oystermen who plied their trade during the day and at night secretly worked flashing colored lights in response to boats carrying fugitives from Dover, Delaware, or other points south. Could this have been the way Hicks found his way to New Jersey, crossing the bay in a boat flashing a signal of lights? Passing Cohansey Creek, they may have been reminded that here, fugitives made their way up to that Quaker stronghold Greenwich/Springtown, where they could feel more than a modicum of safety. As they approached Cape May, they could all gaze at that resort town where Blacks like Harriet Tubman labored during the day for the enjoyment and revelry of wealthy Whites but also may have spied on southerners and politicians for the UGRR. Then at Cape May Point, the

Northward view of the Delaware River with Benjamin Franklin Bridge in background. *Author's photo.*

Cooper Public Library (at the former location of Cooper's Ferry). *Author's photo.*

steamer reached the entrance of the bay and the Atlantic Ocean. Just as they began turning southward, the men could look east and see the lighthouse standing tall as a beacon to not only ships at sea but also fugitives crossing the bay, signaling that they had arrived on free land. The lighthouse was now bidding those soldiers fare-thee-well, just as it had previously welcomed fugitives. Here, the transports were beyond New Jersey and officially below the Mason-Dixon Line at sea; nonetheless, as they steamed into the open waters of the Atlantic, they carried all the spirits of fugitives who fled north to freedom through perilous journeys while suffering untold tribulations. Now, these men were to be the answer to all those wrongs of the past.

Hot Danger

As they steamed south, the Black soldiers felt confident they would make a difference. As far as the U.S. military was concerned, the Black soldiers were adding to the might of the army in total war. Adam Badeau, military secretary and aide-de-camp to Union general Ulysses S. Grant during the Civil War, wrote that Grant believed there could be no holding the peace until the rebels' military power was completely broken. He wrote:

> *This was the primal idea, the cardinal principle with which he began his campaigns as general-in-chief—to employ all the force of all the armies continually and concurrently, so that there should be no recuperation on the part of the rebels, no rest from attack, no opportunity to reinforce first one and then another point with the same troops, at different seasons; no possibility of profiting by the advantages of interior lines; no chance to furlough troops, to reorganize armies, or re-create supplies; no respite of any sort, anywhere, until absolute submission ended the war.*[379]

Black soldiers were increasing the power, size and extent of the U.S. military sufficient to place a stranglehold on the Confederacy. Throughout 1864 and 1865, until the South surrendered, Grant threw all the might of the entire U.S. military at the Confederates, including the Black troops, who were now equipped physically, mentally and spiritually for total war against slavery. Badeau wrote that Grant realized Richmond's strength or weakness lay at Petersburg.[380] Arriving in Virginia—the seat of the Confederacy, flower of the South and esteemed home state of George Washington—the

Twenty-Second Regiment was about to play an instrumental part in the despoliation of the Cavalier code and southern honor.

At first, the soldiers of the Twenty-Second Regiment did duty protecting supply lines, then they were called on to join the fight. According to regiment surgeon James Otis Moore, the regiment began marching toward Richmond on March 1, 1864, at five thirty in the afternoon, in the cold and dark. Another officer reported that they could not see their steps. All the regiments marched all night, stopping only to rest a little.[381] General Butler was in charge of the Army of the James, which worked along with General George Meade's Army of the Potomac. Together, these armies made up the Tenth and Eighteenth Corps. The Twenty-Second Regiment USCT fell under the direction of the Eighteenth Corps, commanded

Union general Ulysses S. Grant, general-in-chief of the armies of the United States. *Courtesy of Library of Congress.*

by Brigadier General Charles G. Paine. Grant ordered Butler to advance along the James River south of Richmond down to Petersburg and position his troops above the city. They were to cut off the railroad line. At that time, most of the rebels were east of Grant on the Rapidan River. Those rebels stationed on the James River numbered only about 7,389 men, and Petersburg only had one regiment. Butler had at Yorktown and Gloucester Point 30,000 soldiers. On April 28, Butler received his final orders and, on May 4, began embarking troops on transports down the York River, past Fortress Monroe and up the James River.[382]

On May 4, Butler's invasion force, made up of about thirty armored war vessels, gunboats, steamboats and transports, steamed up the James River to Bermuda Hundred, where two brigades, one including the Twenty-Second, were landed on Wilson's Wharf.[383] By May 6 or 7, Butler had his troops out trying to cut the railroad lines between Richmond and Petersburg, while Major General August V. Krautz had his cavalry cut off communications between Richmond and Confederate general Pierre G.T. Beauregard. In command of Petersburg was Confederate general George E. Pickett, whose name was ignominiously memorialized in Pickett's Charge at the Battle of Gettysburg. Pickett immediately requested help from Beauregard, but the reply was that Beauregard could not come soon. The apprehension was palpable. Not only were Petersburg's communication lines being cut with Richmond, the town was also besieged by enemy forces and armed Black troops. Frantically, Confederates put out a call for forces from as far away as Florida to rush to Virginia with all urgency. "We are in the very crisis of our fortunes, and want every man," telegraphed Confederate secretary of war James Alexander Seddon to General Beauregard. "This city is in *hot* danger." Seddon cried out for every resource to be brought to bear in this emergency situation.[384]

Unfortunately, Butler misread Beauregard's reaction to Union cavalry and delayed any attempts to take Petersburg, which gave Beauregard time to get reinforcements. Throughout May, the Black troops were called to other duties and to help other regiments. On May 21, that changed: one hundred Confederate cavalry attacked Fort Powhatan in an attempt to cut off Butler's supply line. The Black troops guarding those wagons called out for defense, and troops from the Twenty-Second and other Black regiments rushed from Wilson's Wharf and engaged rebel general Fitzhugh Lee. An officer of the First Regiment recorded the encounter: "He had 2,000 men....We had 1,100 men. He came down with cavalry and charged on our pickets, expecting to cut them off, and then surprise the camp. But he 'reckoned without his host.' The pickets fought him for half an hour and emptied several saddles."[385] The rebels demanded a truce and that the Blacks surrender. They did not. Once the truce ended, both sides began firing, but the rebels flanked both sides of the Union soldiers and gave a "yell," then positioned themselves as if they were about to make a charge. The Black soldiers immediately returned a yell even louder and meaner than the rebels'

Military record: Hicks's promotion to corporal. *National Archives.*

"and poured so much lead among them that they broke and ran like sheep, leaving numbers of dead and wounded on the field."[386] Wilson commented, "In this affair they [the rebels] found a foe worthy of their steel."[387] Union general Edward A. Wild commanded the Black troops and had high praise for their behavior, calling their actions those of veterans.[388] Hicks's courage was apparent and noticed by army officials. After this assault, Private Hicks was promoted to Corporal Hicks on June 10, 1864.[389]

Despite this, newspapers still expressed displeasure over having Black troops fighting. Grant was unfazed by this cynicism and criticism. Soon, the press would turn that criticism to praise. Now Grant proceeded with his plan to take Petersburg. General William Farrar Smith was directed to go to Bermuda Hundred, and from there, Butler sent him to Petersburg with his three infantry divisions and one cavalry division, under General August V. Kautz, which was to threaten rebel works on Norfolk Road. General Edward W. Hinks's division of Black troops, including the Twenty-Second, was positioned to the right of Kautz's men. White troops under General T.H. Brooks followed, with Hinks's troops in the center. Other divisions were to proceed along the Appomattox River and hit City Point Road. Smith's men were to move against the northeast side of Petersburg, from City Point to the Norfolk railroad. This was the plan. Badeau argued that Grant's "total war" plan was coming together like pieces in a puzzle. General William T. Sherman was moving toward Atlanta and the ocean; General David Hunter was in the Shenandoah Valley on operations; General Philip H. Sheridan was advancing north to isolate and destroy the rebel cavalry; and Grant and the rest of the army were moving toward Petersburg.[390]

Grant and the Army of the Potomac moved under cover of darkness right under the noses of Confederates, crossed the Chickahominy River and headed south. By the time General Robert E. Lee discovered they were gone on June 13, he telegraphed Richmond. About midnight on June 15, 1864, Smith's troops were crossing the Appomattox River and Grant's troops were crossing the James River on transports. Lee realized federal troops were moving toward Petersburg. Union forces now needed to make a quick attack.[391] Hinks's three divisions of infantry numbered about 3,500 soldiers, which included Smith's corps and a brigade commanded by Colonel Samuel Duncan that included the Twenty-Second. The corps marched to the northeastern side of Petersburg, about six miles outside the city at Bailey's Farm, where they came into contact with rebel pickets, who fired on them. Kautz's troops reconnoitered the area and found a series of rebel rifle trenches and rebel cavalry and light battery behind the woods. The ground leading up to the works rose three to four hundred yards, with the enemy positioned on high ground in front of the woods, which was swampy with fallen trees. A railroad line and turnpike both crossed it, and the rebel battery lay in an open field with unblocked views in all directions. This was a difficult operation. In order to get to the battery, Union forces had to move out of the woods, run up a slope and take the rebel position at bayonet point, all under deadly gunfire.[392] Smith deployed the troops, with Duncan's brigade in the center. The men passed over the swampy, wooded ground with its tangled vegetation and were confronted by rebel pickets with canister fire as they exited the woods onto open ground. But the troops pushed on without stopping and returned fire. The Fourth and Fifth Regiments tried to reach the rebel battery but could not because of the heavy gunfire. They fell back, then reformed and went back with other troops. The troops could only move at a slow pace and had to keep lying down to avoid the gunfire. After other troops tried assaults, the men in the center, the Twenty-Second and the Fifth on the left, were called to assault. These soldiers rushed forward, made their way up a ravine as rebel shells slammed all around them and, with a "wild cheer," ran up the slope amidst musketry fire. At least 100 men fell, but the troops continued like a cyclone and took the works and the rebel cannon, then used it on the rebels who were fleeing for their lives toward Petersburg and their main entrenchment. "It was the 22nd U.S. Colored Troops that took the works when we fell back, and not the 5th Cavalry," stated Sergeant Major Fleetwood.[393] Badeau wrote that Kiddoo's regiment, "was the first to gain the hill….The rebels, assaulted thus in front and flank, gave way; four of the guns already captured were turned upon them by the negro conquerors, enfilading the line."[394] Kiddoo wrote in his report that the enemy stopped firing artillery as the men crossed the swampy area and manned the rifle pits. The gunfire was so intense that the men of the Twenty-Second waivered at first, but they continued pushing on to reach the battery.[395] Butler described the assault thus: "The strongest of these works was captured by a skirmish line of negro soldiers, and no troops have advanced a step beyond their position in that direction, after seven months of siege."[396] The total lost for the Union forces was 378 men—44 killed, 317 wounded and 17 missing.

The Black soldiers all reveled in the win, and the White soldiers marveled at the feats of the Black soldiers who rushed the rebel battery. When word got out in Petersburg that the rebel soldiers had fled from Black soldiers, the city's White women were told not to trust those soldiers[397]—probably because the women believed those soldiers could not defend them and did not uphold southern honor. The fighting men from South Jersey were the main part of that assault. As Twenty-Second Regiment color-bearer, Salem County resident Edward Richardson participated in the fiercest battles in the Petersburg campaign.[398] He would have been there racing up the slope, carrying the flag and leading on his regiment. Corporal Hicks from Gloucester County would also have participated and been responsible for encouraging his fellow soldiers on toward the rebel battery. Both he and Richardson survived this grueling and dangerous assignment.

The assault gave the colored soldiers some respect from White soldiers. Despite the great victory, General Smith did not follow up and take Petersburg. This failure resulted in Union forces laying siege to the town. Public concern about this failure made Lincoln nervous, so he decided to take a trip to visit Grant and his armies to assuage their fear and to sanction Grant's management of the war. Before going to Virginia, Lincoln attended a public meeting in Philadelphia, where he spoke of his confidence in Grant and made a prediction that the general, along with Pennsylvanian generals George Meade and Winfield Scott Hancock, would not be forced out by rebels but would take Richmond. Then, on June 21, 1864, Lincoln visited Grant's headquarters at City Point. After a private meeting, Lincoln borrowed the general's horse, Cincinnati, and rode out to review Meade and Butler's front line. As he completed his review, he saw the Army of the Potomac and decided to ride through the line and view the Negro troops of the Eighteenth Corps, which had fought courageously and won ground on the first assault on Petersburg. Among the men of the Eighteenth Corps was the Twenty-Second Regiment. Hicks, Richardson, Jackson and all the other men stood at attention while the president reviewed them. A sea of colored men of all complexions stood facing the leader of the United States as he reviewed them. A dark-skinned man standing at five feet, eleven and a half inches tall, Hicks stood out among the group. He would have had a clear view of the president over many of his comrades.[399] Then "they crowded around him, anxious to see the man who had liberated them, and cheers and cries of joy and affection arose on every hand. These men who had been slaves, pressing up in the garb of soldiers, to bless and look upon him who was now *their* President and chief, made a sight to impress the dullest imagination," wrote Badeau. As Lincoln rode among the Black troops, they thronged him, and Lincoln removed his top hat in recognition of their service.[400]

Lincoln's visit boosted the morale of the soldiers and Grant. Now he could continue with his plans. Meade approved a plan to tunnel underneath Confederate lines and plant bombs that would blow up, allowing time for Federal forces to take the enemy's works before Petersburg. On July 30, the

Military record: Hicks's promotion to sergeant. *National Archives.*

big mine, planted with between 1,200 to 1,400 pounds of gunpowder, was blown up. According to Badeau, the explosion went off "with a shock like that of an earthquake, tearing up the rebel works above it, and vomiting earth, men, guns, and caissons, two hundred feet in the air."[401] Union troops were supposed to have rushed in to take the rebel works, but there was a delay, and when the White and Black Union soldiers finally did go into the crater, they were exposed to rebel gunfire from those soldiers who had recovered from the shock. It was a slaughter. The valor and bravery of those Black soldiers did not go unnoticed by Black war correspondent Thomas Morris Chester, who wrote, "For several hundred yards the ground was thickly strewn with debris.…Fragments of humanity were scattered around in the immediate vicinity of the tragedy in frightful profusion. Sorrow was depicted in every countenance that gazed on the ruins, but those loudest in their grief were the contrabands who mourned their relatives and comrades. Being employed in great numbers where the accident occurred, more of them were killed or wounded than any other class of individuals."[402] These Blacks were forced laborers, slaves and freedmen living in the state, conscripted by the Confederate government to construct its trenches and batteries around the city. Most of the forced workers came from Petersburg and Richmond.[403] After the crater explosion, Hicks was promoted again, to sergeant.[404] He had to have played a very significant part and shown great courage and honor in that horrific event.

FOLLOWING THE SIEGE OF Petersburg and crater explosion, the Twenty-Second was involved in assaults at New Market Heights, where soldiers had to cross an open field, go through a wooded area with a steep ravine and creek, cross a swampy area that was within the rebels' firing range and navigate a row of felled trees, or abatis, to take the enemy's earthworks with armed rebels. The men of the Twenty-Second crossed all the rebel defenses but got bogged down at the abatis, which required axmen to cut away at the timber while under fire. Every time one axman was shot down, another took his place. The Black troops finally were able to get through the abatis, then "with a shout that rang out above the roar of artillery," they ran and took the rebel redoubt and engaged the rebels in hand-to-hand combat with bayonets. In this incident, rebels ran away, just like when the Black soldiers rushed the rebel works outside Petersburg, abandoning their cannon and small arms.[405]

Now, with the final defenses around Richmond conquered, Union forces set their faces toward the rebel capitol. When Richmond was finally taken, Chester gave the Black troops their due, which he witnessed in April 1865: "Brevet Brigadier General Draper's brigade of Colored troops, Brevet Major General Kautz's division were the first infantry to enter Richmond."[406] Draper's brigade included the Twenty-Second Regiment. As the Black troops marched victoriously into the rebel capitol, Chester recorded on April 4, 1865, the reaction of the formerly enslaved, who called out, "You've come at

Military record: Hicks's muster-out roll. *National Archives.*

last," "We've been looking for you these many days," "Jesus has opened the way" and "God bless you."[407]

Among those troops were Hicks and Richardson, triumphant and proud. Musicians played "John Brown's Body" as the troops marched into the city. Wilson stated that as they marched, a little girl waved a U.S. flag.[408] This was a significant symbol that the Confederacy was crushed. Hicks must have shown great courage, character and disposition as a soldier with the ability to command men, since he was promoted twice during his service.[409]

After Lincoln was assassinated, the Twenty-Second Regiment USCT was the only Black regiment to participate in the president's funeral procession, and then it was the only Black regiment chosen to pursue the assassin John Wilkes Booth. Hicks would have been one of those chosen for this service. Following the hunt for Booth, Hicks was sent along with the Eighteenth Corps to perform duty along the Rio Grande in Texas. Troops were sent to Texas by General Grant, who expected trouble from Mexico and Confederates in that state. Major General Godfrey Weitzel was ordered to move his Twenty-Fifth Army Corps, which included by this time the Twenty-Second Regiment USCT, to City Point for embarkation, taking with them forty days' rations for twenty thousand men, half of his land transportation and one-fourth of his mules and forage for them.[410] The United States was concerned that the French-installed emperor in Mexico, Maximillian, would try to take advantage of the confusion in Texas with the end of the war and violate the Monroe Doctrine. To warn off Mexican aggression and "to intimidate the French" as well as to put down any ex-Confederate actions the federal troops, including the Twenty-Second Regiment USCT, patrolled the border and made their presence known to all.[411]

Hicks mustered out on October 16, 1865, in Brownsville, Texas. After mustering out, he and others from the Twenty-Second Regiment USCT would have taken a steamer back up to Baltimore and then boarded a train for Camp William Penn. After five days of saying goodbye to comrades and officers, their service was completed, and the soldiers became civilians again.[412] At the end of the war, Hicks returned to his family a hero. Other soldiers of the Twenty-Second Regiment USCT also went home held as heroes in their communities.

REGIMENTAL HISTORY: 22ND REGIMENT INFANTRY USCT

Organized at Philadelphia, Pa., January 10–29, 1864.
Ordered to Yorktown, Va., January , 1864.
Attached to U.S. Forces, Yorktown, Va., Dept. of Virginia and North Carolina, to April, 1864.
1st Brigade, Hincks' Division (Colored), 18th Corps, Army of The James, to June, 1864.
1st Brigade, 3rd Division, 18th Corps, June, 1864.
2nd Brigade, 3rd Division, 18th Corps, to August, 1864.
1st Brigade, 3rd Division, 18th Corps, August, 1864.
1st Brigade, 3rd Division, 10th Corps, to September, 1864.
1st Brigade, 3rd Division, 18th Corps, to December, 1864.
1st Brigade, 3rd Division, 25th Corps, December, 1864.
1st Brigade, 1st Division, 25th Corps, and Dept. of Texas, to October, 1865.

SERVICE—Duty near Yorktown, Va., till May, 1864. Expedition to King and Queen County March 9–12.
Butler's operations south of James River and against Petersburg and Richmond May 4–June 15.
Duty at Wilson's Wharf, James River, protecting supply transports, then constructing works near Fort Powhatan till June. Attack on Fort Powhatan May 21.
Before Petersburg June 15–18. Siege operations against Petersburg and Richmond June 16, 1864, to April 2, 1865.
Deep Bottom August 24. Dutch Gap August 24.
Demonstration north of the James River September 28–30.
Battle of Chaffin's Farm, New Market Heights, September 29–30.

Fort Harrison September 29.

Battle of Fair Oaks October 27–28.

Chaffin's Farm November 4.

In trenches before Richmond till April, 1865.

Occupation of Richmond April 3.

Moved to Washington, D.C., and participated in the obsequies of President Lincoln and afterwards to eastern shore of Maryland and along lower Potomac in pursuit of the assassins.

Rejoined Corps May, 1865.

Moved to Texas May 24–June 6.

Duty along the Rio Grande till October, 1865.

Mustered out October 16, 1865.

Regiment lost during service 2 Officers and 70 Enlisted men killed and mortally wounded and 1 Officer and 144 Enlisted men by disease. Total 217.

Source: Dyer, Compendium.

After the war, General Butler thought men like Hicks were heroes, too. Butler was so impressed with the actions of the Black soldiers around Petersburg and at New Market Heights that he pledged to defend their rights forever. One honor he gave the regiments that participated in those actions was to have their Black regimental flags inscribed with "Petersburg" and "New Market Heights."[413] Another honor Butler performed for those soldiers was to commission and award a special Tiffany silver medal to approximately two hundred soldiers after the war. Called the Butler Medal, it featured an image of Black soldiers charging a battery, with inscriptions on both sides. The soldier's name, company and regiment were also engraved on the rim. The medal hung on a red, white and blue ribbon and included an oak-leaf pin inscribed with "Army of the James."[414] Unfortunately, no lists of medal recipients exist, and the U.S. government did not recognize the Butler Medal.[415] Yet the men who received the medal must have felt proud and appreciated for their service. Black soldiers like Hicks and Richardson also could feel proud of the fact that during the war, fewer than 5 percent of Black soldiers deserted, compared to the White rate, which was over 14 percent.[416]

This medal would have been a big deal for those soldiers who received it, according to Lieutenant Colonel Joseph Winfield Murray III, U.S. Army Signal Corps (retired). In a telephone interview Murray stated, "The

Gravestone for Herney Turner, soldier, Twenty-Second Regiment USCT, in Mt. Pisgah AME Cemetery. *Author's photo.*

Butler Medal was in addition to fourteen Medal of Honors given so, any recognition for Black soldiers was gratefully received." He added, "Butler paid for these medals because of the lack of Black soldier recognition by the army leadership itself." Murray argued that although many Black men received medals, the total number of medal-recognition events held for them during the Civil War was far less than those for their White counterparts. "This injustice remains in standard practice throughout the next century within the U.S. military," Murray stated.[417]

MARL-RICH

Back home, Hicks and his family did not have to fear being returned to slavery anymore. He could live out his life truly a free man on property purchased from Isaac Riley on July 19, 1861, and officially recorded at the Gloucester County Courthouse on August 1, 1861.[418] Hicks's connection to Riley is unclear. They were both Black and from Delaware before moving to New Jersey. Could they have known each other in Delaware? As neighbors in Franklin Township, they lived next to one another before the war. The 1860 Census for the township shows Riley was sixty-four years old and owned real estate valued at $200.[419]

After he was discharged from the army, Tribbitt returned to New Jersey and his family. By 1910, he was married to a woman named Lizzie, and they had two children. The family was living on ten acres of land on Rural Route 1 in Franklinville. Tribbitt was making a living as a farmer and owned his own truck.[420] Hicks and Tribbitt probably knew each other, since they lived close by one another after the war. In all probability, they knew each other at Camp William Penn, and it is highly probable that Tribbitt's injury was known to all the recruits and would have been talked about. Their connection extended unto death. Both soldiers were laid to rest in the same section and block of Green's Cemetery in the Janvier section of Franklin Township. Hicks passed away on May 10, 1905. Tribbitt passed away on August 10, 1915.[421] Brothers in arms if not in action, Hicks and Tribbitt represented the desire of Black Americans to fight for freedom and rights. Their sacrifices brought danger and life-altering injuries. They both manifested potential to develop, achieve and succeed, and they, like all the Black soldiers who enlisted, demonstrated these ideals and proved their manhood. Each man was a hero in a different way. Tribbitt offered his body and received lifelong

200

GRANTEE.		GRANTOR.	BOOK.	PAGE.	DATE	WHEN RECORDED
Hulseman	John	Etal	Edward C. Rice by Shf.	Y4	540	Dec 5. 1863	Dec 17. 1863
Hewlings	Josiah F.		Carleton P. Stokes reife	Y4	28	Jany 30.1861	Jany 31.1861
Hews	James &C			Y4	670	Nov 28 1863	Mch 8.1864
Hampton	James &C		Uriah Smith	Y4	684	Jany 21.1864	Mch 10.1864
Haines	John		Nathan Shute Jr reife	Y4	713	Nov 29. 1858	Mch 21.1864
Hilyard	Jeremiah		Robert Wilson reif	Y4	113	Aug 27. 1860	Oct 24.1861
Hicks	John W		Isaac Riley	Y4	88	July 19. 1861	Aug 1. 1861
Hampton	Jeptha		James A Britten reife Eal	Z4	5	May 22. 1862	June 13.1862
Harr	Jacob		Stille Chew Ree	Z4	602	Sep 3. 1863	Oct 29. 1863
Hoogate	Jeremiah D.	Etal	William Ewley reif.	Z4	606	Oct 28. 1863	Oct 29.1863
Holmes	John		Josiah R Holmes	Z4	481	May 14.1863	June 18.1863
Hampton	James &C	Etal	Abram Inekeep reife	Z4	554	Aple 18. 1863	Oct 5. 1863
Hoogate	Jeremiah D.	Etal	Joshua D Loud reif	Z4	16	June 17. 1862	June 21.1862
Holdcraft	John		John Lafferty by Adm	Z4	410	Feby 28. 1863	Apl 25.1863
	John		Elizabeth Lafferty Ree	Z4	412	Mch 14.1863	Apl 25. 1863
Hoogate	Jeremiah D.	Etal	John M Moore	Z4	167	Dec 30. 1862	Jany 2. 1863
"	Jeremiah D.	Etal	Thomas A Morn	Z4	297	Mch 13. 1863	Mch 15. 1863
	Jeremiah D.		John M. &c	Z4	639	Nov 5 1863	Nov 14.1863
"	Jeremiah D.	Etal	Jacob R Usinger	Z4	37	Aug 5.1862	Aug 13.1863
Haverstraw	Jacob		Susan Vansyckel	Z4	199	Jany 24 1863	Jany 24.1863
Hoogate	Jeremiah D.	Etal	Eli Wilson reife	Z4	34	Aug 4.1862	Aug 6.1862
Horner	Joseph		James Alorn reife	A5	495	Mch 12.1864	June 18.1865
"	Joseph		William Alorn reife	A5	497	Aug 20. 1864	June 10. 1865
Hoffman	James A		Joseph E Haines	A5	64	Mch 8.1862	Feby 10. 1864
Hulings	Jonathan		Biddle Moffett	A5	626	Mch 11. 1865	Sept 6.1865
Hacket	Joseph	Etal	George P. Oliver reife	A5	579	July 24. 1865	Aug 4.1865
Haines	John		Prest Gloucester Co Bank	A5	107	Mch 15. 1864	Apl 6.1864
Hoffman	James A		Thomas S Weatherly reife	A5	137	Mch 19 1864	Apl 16.1864
Harr	Jacob		Eben Whitney reife	A5	617	Mch 25. 1865	Sept 2.1865
Heritage	Jacob		Francis A Campbell by &c	B5	527	Mch 10 1864	Apl 5.1865
Higgins	Joseph		Benjamin H Diltes reif	B5	393	Jany 9. 1865	Jany 26.1865
Haines	John		John M Moore reife Etal	B5	270	Nov 1. 1864	—
Holmes	James E	Etal	Samuel Paul (Heirs of)	B5	606	Mch 21.1865	Apl 20.1865
	John S	Etal	"	B5	606	Mch 21. 1865	Apl 20.1865
	James E	Etal	" by heirs	B5	608	Feby 28.1865	Apl 20.1865
"	John S	Etal	"	B5	608	Feby 28.1865	Apl 20.1865
Harding	Joseph		Anthony Shawer reife	B5	546	Mch 31. 1865	Apl 6.1865
Adams	James E		John Beckett Heirs of &c	C5	337	Dec 16.1865	Mch 6.1866
Hartman	Joseph		Samuel A Darr reife	C5	176	Oct 19.1865	Oct 26 1865
	John		Moses Gibson reife	C5	88	Feby 15.1865	Nov 24.1865

Property sale records, Isaac Riley to John W. Hicks. *Gloucester County Old Courthouse, Office of Records & Deeds.*

PLEASE PRINT OR TYPE **GRAVE REGISTRATION RECORD**

Name Hicks, John W. Serial No.
Home Address
Next of Kin Address
Born At
Date of Death May 10, 1905 Cause
Buried 19 in Green's Cemetery
City Janvier County Gloucester
Division Section A Lot No. 8 Block F Grave No. 4
War Record Civil War
Branch of Service Co. E, 22nd Regt., U.S.C.V. Rank Sgt
Enlisted 4/27/1861 - 12/26/1863 Discharged 7/31/1861 - 10/16/1865
Information Given by Relationship
Remarks Grave in fair condition. Family removed to N. Y.
Care Assigned to Post No.
Government Headstone Desired [ ] Yes [ ] No   Organization Marker Placed [X] Yes [ ] No

PLEASE PRINT OR TYPE **GRAVE REGISTRATION RECORD**

Name Tribbitt, William Serial No.
Home Address
Next of Kin Daughter, Lizzie Williams Address R.F.D. Franklinville, N. J.
Born 1836 At
Date of Death August 10, 1915 Cause
Buried 19 in Green's Cemetery
City Janvier County Gloucester
Division Section A Lot No. 5 Block F Grave No. 3
War Record Civil War
Branch of Service Co. J, 22nd Regt. U.S.C.V. Rank Pvt
Enlisted January 5, 1864 Discharged July 13, 1864
Information Given by Relationship
Remarks Grave in poor condition.
Care Assigned to Post No.
Government Headstone Desired [ ] Yes [ ] No   Organization Marker Placed [X] Yes [ ] No

Hicks and Tribbitt grave registration records, WPA file. *Courtesy of Gloucester County Historical Society.*

injuries; Hicks offered his life and survived deadly battles and the hardships of camp and army life and witnessed the horrors of war. But he lived to tell the tale. These Black men, like all the Black soldiers, dispelled the falsehood that Black men were too weak-minded, scared or uncivilized to train and fight in war. They proved their worth to the Union and their race, showing humanity, courage and determination. And they bequeathed to the generations freedom from slavery. Their sacrifice still inspires and hails from the valiant endeavors of abolitionists and Quakers who refused to comply with slavery's mandates and instead resisted its authority. They proved their salt and helped save a nation.

EPILOGUE

At ten o'clock in the morning on Saturday June 1, 2019, on a warm and beautiful day with a clear blue cloudless sky, a grand rededication ceremony was held at Green's Cemetery in Franklinville to honor the soldiers buried there, including Civil War soldiers Hicks, Tribbitt and Jackson. In attendance were county officials; members of VFW Post 473 of Camden; members of the Gloucester County chapter of the National Association for the Advancement of Colored People (NAACP); reenactors from the Second New Jersey Brigade New Jersey's Civil War Brigade; members of the Buffalo Soldiers Motorcycle Clubs of New Jersey, Pennsylvania, Delaware and New York; a President Abraham Lincoln reenactor; members of the Third Regiment USCT reenactors; Pastor Franklin Gosnell of Emmanuel Baptist Church, Glassboro; students from Gloucester County Institute of Technology; and residents from across the county and state. The event opened with the motorcycle clubs parading down Tuckahoe Road to the cemetery. There, guests, honor guards, reenactors, officials and residents entered and took their places. Then songs were sung, prayers offered, praises raised by officials and speeches given. The U.S. flag and the Twenty-Second USCT regimental flag were presented by the VFW Post members, and after some more speeches and songs, the Civil War reenactors conducted a twenty-one-gun salute. More songs, speeches and remarks came, extolling the courage and commitment of the soldiers. Then the ceremony closed with the retiring of the colors. At least one hundred people attended the ceremony for the soldiers no one there had ever met but nonetheless respected. Some attendees knew family members of the Civil War soldiers but had no idea their ancestors were in the war. Still, everyone at that service paid homage to those men. They were not forgotten. The morning's event was a fitting tribute to those men who sacrificed their lives to free their people and ultimately save a Union.

Green's Cemetery rededication: color guard. *Author's photo*.

Green's Cemetery rededication: county officials. *Author's photo*.

Green's Cemetery rededication: Lincoln reenactor. *Author's photo.*

Green's Cemetery rededication: Twenty-Second Regiment USCT reenactors. *Author's photo*.

Green's Cemetery rededication: reenactor's gun salute. *Author's photo.*

Green's Cemetery rededication: Tribbitt gravestone. *Author's photo.*

Green's Cemetery rededication: Hicks gravestone. *Author's photo.*

Green's Cemetery rededication: Andrew Jackson gravestone. *Author's photo.*

NOTES

Chapter 1

1. Holliday, *Exploring Quakerism*, 1.
2. McCormick, *New Jersey*, 39.
3. Proprietors, *Concessions and Agreements*, 24–25; Gloucester County Historical Society, Woodbury, NJ; Kull, *New Jersey*, 99; Cushing and Sheppard, *Gloucester, Salem, and Cumberland*, 316.
4. Proprietors, *Concessions and Agreements*, 4–6, 13, 24–25; Cushing and Sheppard, *Gloucester, Salem, and Cumberland*, 316.
5. Fishman, *African American Struggle*, 29–30; McCormick, *New Jersey*, 40–41, 47–51.
6. Cushing and Sheppard, *Gloucester, Salem, and Cumberland*, 316; Fishman, *African American Struggle*, 30; Proprietors, *Concessions and Agreements*, 3–6, 15–16.
7. Woodson, *Education of the Negro*, 24, 43–44; Hodges, *Slavery and Freedom*, 26–30.
8. McCormick, *New Jersey*, 51; Fishman, *African American Struggle*, 81–83.
9. Woolman, *Journal*, 32–36.
10. Ibid., 79, 130–133.
11. Hodges, *Slavery and Freedom*, 72, 74.
12. Cooley, *Study of Slavery*, 31.
13. Zilversmit, *First Emancipation*, 5, 13, 17, 19, 23–24.
14. Ibid., 91–92.
15. Aptheker, *Negro*, 6.

16. Holton, *Black Americans*, 5; Price, *Freedom Not Far*, 51; Fishman, *African American Struggle*, 90; Frances D. Pingeon, *Blacks*, 24; Gerlach, *New Jersey*, 87–88.

17. Zilversmit, *First Emancipation*, 140; Sedgwick, *Memoir*, 298–99.

18. Zilversmit, *First Emancipation*, 94; Nash, *Race and Revolution*, 117, 123, 125.

19. *Gloucester County Slavery Book Without a Cover, Manumission Book. Manumission papers for David Cooper and Samuel Allinson. December 22, 1774.* Gloucester County Historical Society, Woodbury, NJ.

20. Haro, "Haddonfield," 342; Lewis, "Indian King Tavern," 405.

21. Gerlach, *New Jersey*, 437; Price, *Freedom Not Far Distant*, 61–62.

22. Dorwart, *Cape May County*, 59.

23. Kull, *New Jersey*, 47.

24. Hagan, Green, Harris and Price, "New Jersey Afro-Americans," 67; Price, *Freedom Not Far Distant*, 53, 63–64.

25. Hodges, *Black New Jersey*, 38–39; Quarles, *Negro in the American Revolution*, 147–48, 174–75; Horton and Horton, *Slavery*, 39–40, 58; Di Ionno, *Guide*, 127–28; Pepe, "Joshua Huddy," 392; Alford, "Colonel Tye," 23.

Chapter 2

26. Du Bois, *John Brown*, 3.

27. Ibid., 64.

28. Wright, "Breaking the Chains," 211.

29. Price, *Freedom Not Far Distant*, 73–75.

30. Dorwart, *Cape May County*, 59–60.

31. Ibid., 9; Stevens, *Cape May County*, 30.

32. Wright, "Breaking the Chains," 211; Zilversmit, *First Emancipation*, 167, 192–93.

33. Price, *Freedom Not Far Distant*, 79–80.

34. Salem Quarterly Meeting (hereafter SQM), *South Jersey Quakers*.

35. Crew, *Black Life*, 23.

36. Kull, *New Jersey*, 48.

37. Clement, *Sketches*, 284–89.

38. Fishman, *African American Struggle*, 156.

39. Ibid., 133; Horton and Horton, *Black Bostonians*, 28.

40. Siebert, *Underground Railroad*, 123–25.

41. *Camden Mail and New Jersey Advertiser*, January 7, 1835. Camden County Historical Society, Camden, NJ.

42. Swisher, *Oliver Wendell Holmes Devise*, 536.

43. *Camden Mail and New Jersey Advertiser*, 1835.

44. Ibid.
45. Powell, *History of Camden County*, 65.
46. Advertisement, *Camden Mail and New Jersey Advertiser*, August 5, 1835.
47. Article, *Camden Mail and General Advertiser*, October 14, 1835. Camden County Historical Society, Camden, NJ.
48. *Constitution, and Farmers' and Mechanics' Advertiser*, December 6, 1836. Gloucester County Historical Society, Woodbury, NJ.
49. Ibid.
50. *Constitution, and Farmers' and Mechanics' Advertiser*, December 13, 1836.
51. Ward, *Autobiography*, 17, 19; Burke, *Samuel Ringgold Ward*, 11.
52. *Camden Mail and General Advertiser*, December 28, 1836.
53. Cooley, *Study of Slavery*, 52.
54. Editorial, *Constitution, and Farmers' and Mechanics' Advertiser*, December 20, 1836.
55. Camden County Historical Society (hereafter CCHS), "Macedonia AME Church."
56. Simpson, *Under Four Flags*, 74.
57. Ibid., 76; Salvini, *Summer City*, 9.
58. Crew, *Black Life*, 7.
59. Ibid., 24; CCHS, "Macedonia AME Church," 4; Salem County, "Thomas Clement Oliver."
60. CCHS, "Macedonia AME Church." 3.
61. CCHS, "Peter Mott House."
62. Whittaker, "S.J. Had Many Stops."
63. Peter Mott House, *Museum*.
64. Ibid.
65. Blockson, *African Americans in Pennsylvania*, 301–2.
66. Peter Mott House, *Museum*; Still, *Underground Railroad*, about the author.
67. Still, *Underground Railroad*, 54–57, 326–27, about the author.
68. Ibid., about the author.
69. Price and Crew, "Abigail Goodwin."
70. Still, *Underground Railroad*, 443.
71. Harper, "South Jersey's Angel," 5.
72. Drayton, *Personal Memoir*, 5.
73. Conkling, *Passenger on the Pearl*, 9, 13, 15; Ricks, *Escape on the Pearl*, 20.
74. Conkling, *Passenger on the Pearl*, 26–27, 29.
75. Corrigan, "Ties That Bind," 84.
76. Remini, *Edge of the Precipice*, 76.
77. Price and Crew, "Set Herself Free."
78. Smedley, *American Negro*, 347–48.
79. Mott, *Selected Letters*, 37.

80. SQM, *South Jersey Quakers*.
81. Morris and Morris, interview.
82. Ibid.; Blockson, *African Americans in Pennsylvania*, 301.
83. Garrison, interview.
84. Siebert, *Underground Railroad*, 124–25.
85. Ibid., 82.
86. Bradford, *Harriet Tubman*, 110.
87. Clinton, *Harriet Tubman*, 24; Dorchester and Caroline Counties, Maryland Driving Tour.
88. Larson, *Bound for the Promised Land*, 66.
89. CCHS, *"Edgewater" at Croft Farm*.
90. Ibid., 6–7.
91. Ibid., 7–8.
92. Simpson, *Under Four Flags*, 3–5.
93. Swedesboro Economic Development Committee, "Stroll Through."

Chapter 3

94. West Cape May Citizens for Good Government, "Architectural & Historic Features."
95. Ibid.; McMahon, *Historic South Jersey Towns*, 163.
96. Longitude and Latitude/GPS Coordinates, "Arlington (VA)"; CoordinatesGPS.info, "Cape May Point."
97. Lurie, *New Jersey Anthology*, 1; Stevens, *History of Cape May County*, 23; Kull, *New Jersey*, 21.
98. McMahon, *Historic South Jersey Towns*, 163; Dorwart, *Cape May County*, 5; National Park Service (hereafter NPS), "Maritime Activities."
99. Dorwart, *Cape May County*, 16; New Bedford Whaling Museum, "Yankee Whaling," 2; New Bedford Whaling Museum, "Life Aboard," 3.
100. Moore, "Early Negro Settlers," 20.
101. NPS, "Maritime Activities," 1; Dorwart, *Cape May County*, 21, 32, 36–38, 43, 55.
102. Dorwart, *Cape May County*, 39; McMahon, *Historic South Jersey Towns*, 157, 159; McManus, *Black Bondage*, 43.
103. White, *Ar'n't I a Woman?*, 112–13, 115, 120; Wright, *Afro-Americans*, 21; Jones, *Labor of Love*, 30; Fox-Genovese, *Within the Plantation Household*, 68.
104. Dorwart, *Cape May County*, 6–7, 22.
105. Cunningham, *This Is New Jersey*, 256.
106. Dorwart, *Cape May County*, 35, 61.
107. Simpson, *Under Four Flags*, 72.
108. Wilson, *Jersey Shore*, 20.

109. Simpson, *Under Four Flags*, 72.
110. Dorwart, *Cape May County*, 277–78.
111. Ibid., 62–63, 66.
112. Moore, *Early Negro Settlers*, 20–21.
113. Dorwart, *Cape May County*, 80–81.
114. Ibid., 84.
115. McMahon, *Historic South Jersey Towns*, 164; Salvini, *Summer City*, 9.
116. McMahon, *Historic South Jersey Towns*, 164; *Book of Cape May*, 60.
117. Alexander, *Ho! For Cape Island!*, 62–64.
118. Salvini, *Summer City*, 16.
119. *Cape May Star and Wave*, "Baltimorean Recalls Old Days of Steamer Trips to Cape May," October 28. Cape May County Historical and Genealogical Society (hereafter CMCHGS).
120. Ibid.
121. Augustine, "From Refuge to Resort."
122. Boyer, "Old Cape May County," 73.
123. McMahon, *Historic South Jersey Towns*, 164.
124. Ibid., 164–65.
125. Salvini, *Summer City*, 18.
126. Boyer, *Cape May County Story*, 76; Salvini, *Summer City*, 22; *Book of Cape May*, 69.
127. Salvini, *Summer City*, 22; *Book of Cape May*, 70.
128. McMahon, *Historic South Jersey Towns*, 167.
129. Alexander, *Ho! For Cape Island*, 82.
130. *Book of Cape May*, 67–68.
131. Boyer, *Cape May County Story*, 74; Salvini, *Summer City*, 22; Wilson, *Jersey Shore*, 71.
132. Wilson, *Jersey Shore*, 69; Salvini, *Summer City*, 24.
133. McMahon, *Historic South Jersey Towns*, 166; Wilson, *Jersey Shore*, 27–28.
134. Brands, *Heirs of the Founders*, 2, 83, 326.
135. Wilson, *Jersey Shore*, 28; Alexander, *Ho! For Cape Island!*, 81, 115.
136. Mickle, *Gentleman of Much Promise*, vol. 1, xiii–xvii.
137. Ibid., vol. 2, 384.
138. Ibid., vol. 1, 186.
139. Ibid., vol. 2, 384–85.
140. Dorwart, *Cape May County*, 106; Alexander, *Ho! For Cape Island!*, 77.
141. Dorwart, *Cape May County*, 106.
142. Alexander, *Ho! For Cape Island!*, 83.
143. Clinton, *Road to Freedom*, 34.
144. Ibid., 35–38; Bradford, *Harriet Tubman*, 28–30.
145. Tobin and Dobard, *Hidden in Plain View*, 147–50.

146. Clinton, *Harriet Tubman*, 28–31.
147. Du Bois, *Gift of Black Folk*, 73–74.
148. Clinton, *Harriet Tubman*, 34.
149. Bradford, *Harriet Tubman*, 67–68.
150. Bradford, *Scenes in the Life*, 19.
151. Measday, "Cape May," 144; Bradford, *Scenes in the Life*, 20.
152. McGowan and Kashatus, *Harriet Tubman*, 23–25.
153. Foner, *Gateway to Freedom*, 155.
154. Bradford, *Moses of Her People*, 44–45.
155. Foner, *Gateway to Freedom*, 155.
156. Bradford, *Moses of Her People*, 112.
157. Ibid., 114–15.
158. Clinton, *Road to Freedom*, 142.
159. American Colonization Society (hereafter ACS), *Thirty-First Annual Report*; McMahon, *Historic South Jersey Towns*, 166.
160. ACS, *Thirty-First Annual Report*, 20.
161. Klein, "New Jersey Colonization Society," 1, 3–5.
162. Bradford, *Moses of Her People*, 113.
163. Clinton, *Road to Freedom*, 86; Bond, *Hidden History of South Jersey*, 110.
164. Painter, *Sojourner Truth*, 201.
165. Olwell, "Loose, Idle and Disorderly," 99–100, 106.
166. Fox-Genovese, *Within the Plantation Household*, 159–60.
167. Chesnut, *Diary from Dixie*, 222.
168. Ibid., 38.
169. *Pro-Slavery Argument*, 57.
170. Clinton, *Road to Freedom*, 165–66.
171. Fishel, *Secret*, 1, 3, 5.
172. Sizer, "Acting Her Part," 115.
173. Dorwart, *Cape May County*, 99.
174. Knapp, *New Jersey Politics*, 42.
175. Potter, *Impending Crisis*, 1–2, 13.
176. Goldfield, "Antebellum Washington in Context," 3.
177. Taylor, *Philadelphia in the Civil War*, 9–11.
178. Knapp, *New Jersey Politics*, 8.
179. Potter, *Impending Crisis*, 131.
180. Sizer, "Acting Her Part," 118.
181. DeGrave, *Swindler, Spy, Rebel*, 98.
182. Leonard, *All the Daring*, 70.
183. Dorwart, *Cape May County*, 83; Hodges, *Black New Jersey*, 94; Moore, *Early Negro Settlers*, 21.
184. Blockson, *African Americans in Pennsylvania*, 129.

185. Harriet Tubman Museum, "Stephen Smith."
186. Blockson, *African Americans in Pennsylvania*, 52; Harriet Tubman Museum, "Banneker House" and "Stephen Smith."
187. Cape May County Board of Chosen Freeholders, "Historic Sites Map."
188. Dreyfuss, "Stephen Smith."
189. Towns, interview.
190. Taylor, *Cavalier and Yankee*, 147–48, 204–5.
191. Alexander, *Ho! For Cape Island!*, 117.
192. Ibid., 117.
193. Bond, *Hidden History of South Jersey*, 111.
194. Still, *Underground Railroad*, 349–50.
195. Ibid., 382–83.
196. Mid-Atlantic Center for the Arts, "Questions Most Often Asked."
197. Carter and Carter, *Champion of Freedom*.
198. Bond, *Hidden History of South Jersey*, 117.
199. Ibid., 118.
200. Carter and Carter, *Champion of Freedom*.
201. Seward House, *Meet an American Hero*.
202. Ibid. (tour); Carter, interview.
203. Carter and Carter, *Champion of Freedom*.

Chapter 4

204. Paine, *Common Sense*, 5.
205. Price, *Freedom Not Far Distant*, 95.
206. Ibid., 95.
207. Franklin and Moss, *From Slavery to Freedom*, 8–9.
208. Ibid., 12, 22–23.
209. Ibid., 2–3.
210. Price, *Freedom Not Far Distant*, 97–98.
211. Woodson, *Education of the Negro*, 258.
212. New Jersey Colonization Society (hereafter NJCS), *Proceedings*, 3, 5.
213. Ibid., 5.
214. Ibid., 12, 15.
215. Ibid., 23.
216. American Colonization Society, *Twenty-Ninth Annual Report*,
217. NJCS, *Proceedings*, 16–17.
218. Ibid., 19–20.
219. Ibid., 17.
220. Ibid., 20.
221. Davis, "Political Oligarchy," 41–42, 44.

222. Mickle, *Gentleman of Much Promise*, 246.
223. Mickle, *Gentleman of Much Promise*, 114.
224. *Camden Mail and New Jersey Advertiser*, July 22, 1835.
225. Blackwell, "David Naar," 555.
226. Knapp, *New Jersey Politics*, 52.
227. Ibid., 52–53.
228. Ibid., 53–54.

Chapter 5

229. Paine, *Common Sense*, 19.
230. Du Bois, *Gift of Black Folk*, 51.
231. Price, *Freedom Not Far Distant*, 88–89.
232. Ibid.
233. American Colonization Society, *Twenty-Ninth Annual Report*, 13.
234. Woodson, *Education of the Negro*, 259–60.
235. Child, *Appeal*, 123–25.
236. Ibid., 9.
237. Kaplan, *Lincoln and the Abolitionists*, 191.
238. Price, *Freedom Not Far Distant*, 91.
239. New Jersey Writer's Project, *Proceedings*, xli.
240. Price, *Freedom Not Far Distant*, 90.
241. Wolinetz, "New Jersey Slavery," 2254–55.
242. Johnson, "South Jersey Women."
243. Ibid.
244. Price, *Freedom Not Far Distant*, 91.
245. Jackson, *New Jerseyans*, 18.
246. "African American Registry."
247. Jackson, "From South Jersey Roots."
248. Price and Crew, "Poet Hetty Saunders" and "Thomas Clement Oliver."
249. Price and Crew, *Thomas Clement Oliver*.
250. Wright, *Education of Negroes*, 25.
251. Woodson, *Education of the Negro*, 100.
252. Jackson, *From South Jersey Roots*, 1, 6.
253. "African American Registry," 1.
254. Jackson, *From South Jersey Roots*, 6.
255. Price, *Freedom Not Far Distant*, 120–21.
256. Horton, *Black Bostonians*, 59–60.
257. Ibid., 59–60.
258. Goodwin, *Team of Rivals*, 293, 323.
259. Cunningham, *New Jersey America's Main Road*, 177.

260. Scovel, *Three Speeches*, 24.
261. Ibid., 25.
262. Ibid., 16.
263. Ibid., 18.
264. New Jersey Commissioners, *Report of the Commissioners*, 3–7.
265. Ibid., 5–7.
266. Scovel, *Three Speeches*, 25.
267. Ibid., 15–16.
268. Ibid., 17.
269. General Assembly of the State of New Jersey, *Minutes of Votes*, 301–2.
270. Ibid., 363, 365, 368, 448.
271. Knapp, *New Jersey Politics*, 92.
272. Ibid., 92–93.
273. Ohio History Central, "Peace Democrats."
274. Kingseed, "Fire in the Rear," 1.
275. Cunningham, *New Jersey*, 171.
276. Knapp, *New Jersey Politics*, 95.
277. Cunningham, *New Jersey*, 182–83.
278. Ibid., 147.
279. Cooper, *Death of Slavery*, 4.
280. Ibid., 2.
281. Ibid., 2.
282. Ibid., 3.
283. McDougall, *Throes of Democracy*, 454.
284. Franklin and Moss, *From Slavery to Freedom*, 204–5.
285. Perry, *Letters*, 57–59.
286. Ibid., 59.
287. Ibid., 60.
288. Ibid., 60–69.
289. Ibid., 5.
290. Cunningham, *New Jersey*, 184.
291. Foner, *Fiery Trial*, 154–55; McPherson, *Battle Cry of Freedom*, 193.
292. Knapp, *New Jersey Politics*, 51.
293. Greene, "Civil War," 145–46.
294. Worton et al., *New Jersey: Past and Present*, 79.
295. Greene, "Civil War,", 145–46.
296. Foner, *Fiery Trial*, 155.
297. Knapp, *New Jersey Politics*, 51.
298. Davis and Wiley, *Civil War Times*, 19.
299. Goodwin, *Team of Rivals*, 310.
300. Continental Congress, *Observations*, 86, 96–98, 118–120, 122.

Chapter 6

301. Child, *Letters*, 161.
302. Answers.com, "Militia Act of 1862," 1.
303. National Archives, *War Department General Order*, 1.
304. Trevelyan, *American Revolution*, 30–31.
305. Douglass, *Life and Times of Frederick Douglass*, 253.
306. Leland, *Abraham Lincoln*, 124, 129, 133.
307. Wilson, *Black Phalanx*, 315–16.
308. Ibid., 317–18.
309. Ibid., 318–19.
310. Ibid., 319.
311. Taylor, *Philadelphia*, 186–87.
312. Gooch, *Hinsonville's Heroes*, 55, 61.
313. Shaffer, *After the Glory*, 170.
314. Taylor, *Philadelphia*, 187.
315. Gooch, *Hinsonville's Heroes*, 60.
316. Ibid., 187–88.
317. Conrad, "Camp William Penn 1863."
318. Conrad, "Lucretia Mott."
319. Taggart, *Free Military School*, 5.
320. Ibid., 6.
321. Ibid., 9–11.
322. Wilson, *Black Phalanx*, 169.
323. Ibid., 170, 175.
324. Taylor, *Philadelphia*, 239.
325. Ibid., 241.
326. Ibid., 187–88.
327. Scott, *Camp William Penn*, 19.
328. McPherson, *Atlas*, 74.
329. Ibid., 74, 76–77, 139; Scott, *Camp William Penn*, 19.
330. Scott, *Camp William Penn*, 19.
331. Boatner, *Civil War Dictionary*, 458–59; McPherson, *Atlas*, 65, 73, 78–79, 80–83, 112–15.
332. Davis and Wiley, *Civil War Album*, 315.
333. McPherson, *Atlas*, 80.
334. Ibid., 82–83; Davis and Wiley, *Civil War Album*, 322.
335. Taylor, *Philadelphia in the Civil War*, 188.
336. Ibid., 188.
337. Ibid., 189.
338. Horton and Horton, *Black Bostonians*, 119.

339. McDougall, *Throes of Democracy*, 366.

340. Franklin and Moss, *From Slavery to Freedom*, 195; Swisher, *Oliver Wendell Holmes Devise*, 631–32.

341. Swisher, *Oliver Wendell Holmes Devise*, 632.

342. Lurie and Mappen, *Encyclopedia of New Jersey*, 330; Bilby, *Forgotten Warriors*, 10–11.

343. Parker, *Speech*, 1.

344. Ibid., 2.

345. Ibid., 2–3.

346. Jackson, *New Jerseyans*, 146.

347. Russell, "Negro Troops," 191, 198.

348. Scott, *Camp William Penn*, 53.

349. Ibid., 48.

350. Bowell, "Second NJ Brigade."

351. Skinner, *Black Civil War Soldiers*.

352. "Township of Franklin Residents."

353. Skinner, *Black Civil War Soldiers*.

354. National Archives, "Hicks, John W."

355. U.S. Bureau of the Census, U.S. Census, 1860.

356. Skinner, *Black Civil War Soldiers*.

357. National Archives, "Tribit, William."

358. U.S. Bureau of the Census, U.S. Census, 1860.

359. Ibid.

360. National Park Service, "William Tribit."

361. National Archives, "Tribit, William."

362. Ibid.

363. Ibid.

364. Ibid.

365. Schiavo, Franklin Township," 289.

366. Simpson, *Under Four Flags*, 88–89; *American Heritage*, new college edition, s.v. "Marl."

367. U.S. Bureau of the Census, U.S. Census, 1860, State of New Jersey.

368. Paradis, *Strike the Blow*.

369. Ibid., 28–29.

370. Bilby, *Forgotten Warriors*, 26.

371. Muster and Descriptive Roll of a Detachment of United States 22nd Regiment USCT, *James Still*, January 1865, Folder 19, New Jersey State Archives, Trenton, NJ.

372. Wilson, *Black Phalanx*, 132.

373. Higginson, *Army Life*, 9–10, 12–13, 36, 42.

374. Ibid., 38, 42, 75.

375. Scott, *Camp William Penn*, 79; Skinner, *Black Civil War Soldiers.*

376. Scott, *Camp William Penn*, 73.

377. National Park Service, "Andrew Jackson"; Paradis, *Strike the Blow*, 109.

378. Price, *Freedom Not Far Distant*, 73–74.

379. Badeau, *Military History*, 9–10.

380. Ibid., 243.

381. Trudeau, *Like Men of War*, 204–5.

382. Wilson, *Black Phalanx*, 384–85; Badeau, *Military History*, 243–44, 247–48.

383. Wilson, *Black Phalanx*, 385; Badeau, *Military History*, 248.

384. Badeau, *Military History*, 248–51.

385. Badeau, *Military History*, 252–53; Trudeau, *Like Men of War*, 217.

386. Trudeau, *Like Men of War*, 218–19.

387. Wilson, *Black Phalanx*, 393.

388. Ibid.

389. National Archives, "Hicks, John W."

390. Wilson, *Black Phalanx*, 397–398; Badeau, *Military History*, 342, 346–47.

391. Badeau, *Military History*, 347, 349.

392. NPS, "United States Colored Troops"; Trudeau, *Like Men of War*, 221; Badeau, *Military History*, 357; Wilson, *Black Phalanx*, 398.

393. Badeau, *Military History*, 358–59; Wilson, *Black Phalanx*, 401; Trudeau, *Like Men of War*, 222.

394. Badeau, *Military History*, 359.

395. NPS, "United States Colored Troops," 3.

396. Butler, *Speech*, 13.

397. Trudeau, *Like Men of War*, 226; Wilson, *Black Phalanx*, 405–6.

398. Scott, *Camp William Penn*, 79.

399. National Archives, "Hicks, John W."

400. Badeau, *Military History*, 380–82; Philip B. Kunhardt, Jr., Philip B. Kunhardt III, and Peter W. Kunhardt, *Lincoln, foreword by David Herbert Donald, contributing writer, Daniel Terris* (New York: Alfred A. Knopf, 1992), 242.

401. Badeau, *Military History*, 478.

402. Chester, *Dispatches*, 96.

403. NPS, "African Americans."

404. National Archives, "Hicks, John W."

405. Wilson, *Black Phalanx*, 435.

406. Chester, *Dispatches*, 289.

407. Ibid., 290.

408. Wilson, *Black Phalanx*, 456.

409. National Archives, "Hicks, John W."

410. Wilson, *Black Phalanx*, 461.

411. Bowell, "Second NJ Brigade."

412. Paradis, *Strike the Blow*, 241.
413. Ibid., 186.
414. Trudeau, *Like Men of War*, 300.
415. Washington, *Union County's Black Soldiers*, 43–44.
416. Shaffer, *After the Glory*, 16.
417. Murray, interview.
418. Gloucester County Old Courthouse, "John W. Hicks."
419. U.S. Bureau of the Census, U.S. Census, 1860. Franklin Township.
420. Betty Bajewicz Historical Center, Gloucester County file—Census of 1910.
421. Gloucester County Historical Society, Registration Record.

WORKS CITED

A Book of Cape May, New Jersey. Cape May, NJ: Albert Hand, 1937.

"African American Registry." *John Rock, Lawyer, and Abolitionist.* HTML document, accessed 2021. Salem County Historical Society, Salem, NJ.

Alexander, Robert Crozer. *Ho! For Cape Island! 1796–1856.* Cape May, NJ: Edward Stern, 1956.

Alford, Ellen D. "Was 'Colonel Tye' at the Hancock House Massacre?" *Vineland Historical Magazine* 91 (2020).

American Colonization Society. *Thirty-First Annual Report of the American Colonization Society* […]. Washington, D.C.: American Colonization Society, 1848. Available at http://www.ia802503.us.archive.org/33/items/ASPC0001925300/ASPC0001925300.pdf.

———. *Twenty-Ninth Annual Report.* Washington, D.C.: American Colonization Society, 1846. Available at https://archive.org//ia801300.us.archive.org/16/items/annualreportofan00mer_11/annualreportofan00mer-11.pdf.

Answers.com. "What Was the Militia Act of 1862?" Accessed January 13, 2020. https://www.answers.com/Q/What_was_the_Militia_Act_of_1862.

Aptheker, Herbert. *The Negro in the American Revolution.* New York: International Publishers, 1940.

Augustine, William E. "From Refuge to Resort." *Jerseyana*, February 26, 1976. Cape May County Historical and Genealogical Society.

Badeau, Adam. *Military History of Ulysses S. Grant from April, 1861 to April 1865.* Vol. 2. New York: D. Appleton, 1881.

Betty Bajewicz Historical Center. Franklin Township. Gloucester County file—Census of 1910. Franklin Township Historical Advisory Committee.

Bilby, Joseph G. *Forgotten Warriors: New Jersey's African American Soldiers in the Civil War.* Hightstown, NJ: Longstreet House, 1993.

Blackwell, Jon. "David Naar." In *Encyclopedia of New Jersey*, edited by Maxine N. Lurie and Marc Mappen. New Brunswick, NJ: Rutgers University Press, 2005.

Blockson, Charles L. *African Americans in Pennsylvania: Above Ground and Underground.* Harrisburg, PA: RB Books, 2001.

———. *African Americans in Pennsylvania: A History and Guide.* Baltimore, MD: Black Classic Press, 1994.

Boatner, Mark M., III. *The Civil War Dictionary.* New York: David McKay, 1988.

Bond, Gordon. *Hidden History of South Jersey: From the Capitol to the Shore.* Charleston, SC: The History Press, 2013.

Bowell, Robert. "History of the 22nd USCT. The 22nd United States Colored Troops." In *The Second NJ Brigade: New Jersey's Civil War Brigade* (brochure).

Boyer, George F. "Old Cape May County." In *Cape May County Story Book 1.* Wildwood, 1975.

Bradford, Sarah. *Harriet Tubman: The Moses of Her People.* Bedford, MA: Applewood Books, 1886.

———. *Scenes in the Life of Harriet Tubman.* New York: Black Heritage Library Collection Books for Libraries Press, [1869] 1971.

Brands, H.W. *Heirs of the Founders: The Epic Rivalry of Henry Clay, John Calhoun and Daniel Webster, the Second Generation of American Giants.* New York: Doubleday, 2018.

Burke, Ronald K. *Samuel Ringgold Ward: Christian Abolitionist.* Edited by Graham Hodges. New York: Garland, 1995.

Butler, Benjamin F. *Speech of Maj.-Gen. Benj. F. Butler, Upon the Campaign Before Richmond 1864 Delivered at Lowell, Mass.* Boston: Wright & Potter, 1865.

Camden County Historical Society (CCHS). *"Edgewater" at Croft Farm.* African-American History/Underground Railroad Sites Tour/Brochure. Camden: CCHS, October 19, 2013.

———. "Macedonia AME Church." *African-American History/Underground Railroad Sites Tour/Brochure.* Camden: CCHS, October 19, 2013.

———. "Peter Mott House." *African-American History/Underground Railroad Sites Tour/Brochure.* Camden: CCHS, October 19, 2013.

Camden Mail and General Advertiser. January 7, July 22, August 5, October 14 and December 28, 1835.

Cape May County Board of Chosen Freeholders. "Historic Sites Map of Cape May County, NJ." Cape May County Department of Tourism, Historic Sites Map of Cape May County, NJ: African Methodist Episcopal Church.

Cape May Star and Wave. "Baltimorean Recalls Old Days of Steamer Trips to Cape May." October 28, 1954.

Carter, Christine P. Interview by Ellen D. Alford. Tour coordinator, Harriet Tubman Home, Auburn, NY. October 2009.

Carter, Paul G., and Christine P. Carter. *A Champion of Freedom: Harriet Tubman, Liberator, Soldier Missionary.* Compiled by Christine P. Carter. Auburn, NY: Harriet Tubman Home.

Cherey, Ramona. Interview by Ellen D. Alford. Church interpreter, Macedonia AME, Camden. October 19, 2013.

Chesnut, Mary Boykin. *A Diary from Dixie* […]. Gloucester, MA: Peter Smith, 1961.

Chester, Thomas Morris. *Thomas Morris Chester, Black Civil War Correspondent: His Dispatches from the Virginia Front.* Baton Rouge: Louisiana State University Press, 1989.

Child, Lydia Maria. *An Appeal in Favor That Class of Americans Called Africans.* New York: Arno Press and the *New York Times*, [1836] 1968.

Child, Lydia Maria, John G. Whittier and Wendell Phillips. *Letters of Lydia Maria Child with a Biographical Introduction by John G. Whittier.* New York: Negro Universities Press, [1883] 1969.

Clement, John. *Sketches of the First Emigrant Settlers in Newton Township, Old Gloucester County, West New Jersey.* Camden, NJ: Sinnickson Chew, [1877] 1974.

Clinton, Catherine. *Harriet Tubman, The Road to Freedom.* New York: Little, Brown, 2004.

Conkling, Winifred. *Passenger on the Pearl: The True Story of Emily Edmonson's Flight from Slavery.* Chapel Hill, NC: Algonquin Young Readers, 2015.

Conrad, Steve. "Camp William Penn 1863." In *Historic La Mott and Camp William Penn This Country's First Federal Recruiting and Training Camp for Black Soldiers.* La Mott, PA: Citizens for the Restoration of Historic La Mott.

———. "Lucretia Mott: The Village's Spiritual Leader; Camp William Penn and the Civil War." In *Historic La Mott and Camp William Penn This Country's First Federal Recruiting and Training Camp for Black Soldiers.* La Mott, PA: Citizens for the Restoration of Historical La Mott.

Constitution, and Farmers' and Mechanics' Advertiser. December 6, 13 and 20, 1836.

Continental Congress. *Observations on the American Revolution* […]. Manifesto, PA: Styner and Cist, 1779.

Cooley, Henry Scofield. *A Study of Slavery in New Jersey (1896).* Fourteenth Series 9–10, Johns Hopkins University Studies in Historical and Political Science. Edited by Herbert B. Adams. Baltimore, MD: Johns Hopkins Press, 1896.

Cooper, Peter. *The Death of Slavery: Letter from Peter Cooper to Governor Seymour, His Excellency Horatio Seymour, Governor of the State of New York.* No. 28. New York: Loyal Publication Society, 1863. Available at https://archive.org/details/deathofslaveryle00coop/.

CoordinatesGPS.info. "Coordinates and Cape May Point Map—Latitude and Longitude." Accessed July 15, 2019. https://gpscoordinates.info/state/new-jersey/cape-may/cape-may-point/.

Corrigan, Mary Beth. "The Ties That Bind: The Pursuit of Community and Freedom among Slaves and Free Blacks in the District of Columbia, 1850–1860." In *Southern City, National Ambition: The Growth of Early Washington, D.C., 1860–1920.*, edited by Howard Gillette Jr. Washington, D.C.: George Washington University Center for Washington Area Studies, 1995.

Crew, Spencer R. *Black Life in Secondary Cities: A Comparative Analysis of the Black Communities of Camden and Elizabeth, N.J. 1860–1920.* New York: Garland, 1993.

Cunningham, Barbara, ed. *The New Jersey Ethnic Experience.* Union City, NJ: Wm. A. Wise, 1977.

Cunningham, John T. *New Jersey: America's Main Road.* New York: Doubleday, 1966.
———. *This Is New Jersey.* 3rd ed. New Brunswick, NJ: Rutgers Univesity Press, 1978.

Cushing, Thos., and Charles E. Sheppard. *History of the Counties of Gloucester, Salem, and Cumberland.* Philadelphia: Everts & Peck, 1883.

Davis, William C., and Bell L. Wiley. *Civil War Times Illustrated Civil War Album Complete Photographic History of the Civil War Fort Sumter to Appomattox.* New York: Tess Press, 1984.

DeGrave, Kathleen. *Swindler, Spy, Rebel: The Confidence Women in Nineteenth Century America.* Columbia: University of Missouri Press, 1995.

Di Ionno, Mark. *A Guide to New Jersey's Revolutionary War Trail for Families and History Buffs.* New Brunswick, NJ: Rutgers University Press, 2000.

Dorchester and Caroline Counties. Maryland Driving Tour. Poplar Neck. Madison. *Finding a Way to Freedom, Harriet Tubman and the Underground Railroad.* Brochure & map. Heart of the Chesapeake Country Heritage Area. https://visitdorchester.org.

Dorwart, Jeffrey M. *Cape May County, New Jersey: The Making of an American Resort Community.* New Brunswick, NJ: Rutgers University Press, 1993.

Douglass, Frederick. *The Life and Times of Frederick Douglass, with an Introduction by Rayford W. Logan.* Mineola, NY: Dover, [1881] 2003.

Drayton, Daniel. *Personal Memoir of Daniel Drayton, for Four Years and Four Months a Prisoner (For Charity's Sake) in Washington Jail, Including a Narrative of the Voyage and Capture of the Schooner Pearl.* New York: Negro Universities Press, [1855] 1969.

Dreyfuss, Barbara. "Stephen Smith: Cape May's Underground Railroad Leader." Capemaymag.com. Fall 2015. http://www.StephenSmith_CapeMay'sUndergroundRailroadLeader-capemaymag.com.

Du Bois, W.E.B. *The Gift of Black Folk: The Negroes in the Making of America.* Edited by Carl A. Anderson. Garden City, NY: Square One, [1924] 2009.

———. *John Brown.* Edited by David Roediger. New York: Modern Library, [1909] 2001.

Dyer, Frederick H. *A Compendium of the War of the Rebellion Compiled and Arranged from Official Records of the Federal and Confederate Armies.* Des Moines, IA: Dyer, 1908.

Elmer, Lucius Q.C., and John T. Nixon. *A Digest of the Laws of New Jersey.* Bridgeton, NJ: State Legislature, 1861.

Fishel, George. *The Secret War for the Union: The Untold Story of Military Intelligence in the Civil War.* Boston: Houghton Mifflin, 1996.

Fishman, George. *The African American Struggle for Freedom and Equality: The Development of a People's Identity, New Jersey, 1624–1850.* New York: Garland, 1997.

Foner, Eric. *The Fiery Trial: Abraham Lincoln and American Slavery.* New York: W.W. Norton, 2010.

———. *Gateway to Freedom: The Hidden History of the Underground Railroad.* New York: W.W. Norton, 2015.

Fox-Genovese, Elizabeth. *Within the Plantation Household: Black & White Women of the Old South.* Chapel Hill: University of North Carolina Press, 1988.

Franklin, John Hope, and Alfred A. Moss Jr. *From Slavery to Freedom: A History of African Americans.* 7th ed. New York: McGraw-Hill, 1994.

Garrison, Lisa. Interview by Ellen D. Alford. *"Caviar Point."* Greenwich, NJ. September 6, 2014).

———. Interview by Ellen D. Alford. *Tour lecturer* Greenwich, NJ, (September 6, 2014).

———. "Tour lecturer." *South Jersey Quakers and the Underground Railroad.* Greenwich, NJ: Salem Quarterly Meeting (SQM), 2014.

General Assembly of the State of New Jersey. *Minutes of Votes and Proceedings of the Eighty-Seventh General Assembly.* Hackensack, NJ: Eben Winton, 1863. New Jersey State Library Collection, Trenton, NJ.

Gerlach, Larry R., ed. *New Jersey in the American Revolution, 1763–1783: A Documentary History.* Trenton: New Jersey Historical Commission, 1975.

Gloucester County File, Census of 1910. Franklinville: Franklin Township Historical Advisory Committee.

Gloucester County Historical Society. Woodbury, NJ. Registration Record. Grave Records File—For Soldiers Serving in the: Indian, Revolutionary, Whiskey Rebellion, War of 1812, Mexican, & Civil Wars. Recorded by the Works Project Administration (WPA) in the 1930s.

Gloucester County Old Courthouse. Woodbury, Gloucester County, New Jersey. August 1, 1861. Office of Records and Deeds. For John W. Hicks. Grantee Index-H. Page 200. Deed Book. Y4. Pages 88–89.

Goldfield, David R. "Antebellum Washington in Context: The Pursuit of Property and Identity." In *Southern City, National Ambition: The Growth of Early*

Washington, D.C. Edited by Howard Gillette Jr. Washington, D.C.: George Washington University Center for Washington Area Studies, 1995.

Gooch, Cheryl Renee. *Hinsonville's Heroes: Black Civil War Veterans.* Lawrence: University Press of Kansas, 2004.

Goodwin, Doris Kearns. *Team of Rivals: The Political Genius of Abraham Lincoln.* New York: Simon & Schuster, 2005.

Gould, Virginia Meacham. "If I Can't Have My Rights, I Can Have My Pleasures, and If They Won't Give Me Wages, I Can Take Them." In *Gender and Slave Labor in Antebellum New Orleans*, in *Discovering the Women in Slavery: Emancipating Perspectives on the American Past*, edited by Patricia Morton. Athens: University of Georgia Press, 1996.

Grave Records File—For Soldiers Serving in the: Indian, Revolutionary, Whiskey Rebellion, War of 1812, Mexican, & Civil Wars. Grave Registration Record, Woodbury: Works Project Administration, 1930s.

Greene, Larry. "Civil War and Reconstruction State and Nation Divided." In *New Jersey: A History of the Garden State*, edited by Maxine L. Lurie and Richard Veit. New Brunswick, NJ: Rutgers University Press, 2015.

Hagan, Lee, Larry A. Greene, Leonard Harris and Clement A. Price. "New Jersey Afro-Americans: From Colonial Times to the Present." In *The New Jersey Ethnic Experience*, edited by Barbara Cunningham. Union City, NJ: Wm. A. Wise, 1977.

Haro, Joseph. "Haddonfield." In *Encyclopedia of New Jersey*, edited by Maxine N. Lurie and Marc Mappen. New Brunswick, NJ: Rutgers University Press, 2005.

Harper, Robert W. "South Jersey's Angel to Runaway Slaves: She Helped to Run the Underground Railroad." *South Jersey Living Magazine of the Sunday Press*, June 15, 1975.

Harriet Tubman Museum, comp. "Banneker House." Display. Cape May, NJ: Harriet Tubman Museum.

———. "Stephen Smith." Display. Cape May, NJ: Harriet Tubman Museum.

Hicks, John W. Gloucester County Old Courthouse, Office of Records and Deeds, Woodbury August 1, 1861.

Higginson, Thomas Wentworth. *Army Life in a Black Regiment.* Edited by Howard N. Meyer. Collier Books, [1862] 1969.

Hodges, Graham Russell. *Black New Jersey: 1664 to the Present Day.* New Brunswick, NJ: 2019.

———. *Slavery and Freedom in the Rural North: African Americans in Monmouth County, New Jersey, 1665–1865.* Madison, WI: 1997.

Holliday, Marsha D. *Exploring Quakerism: A Study Guide.* Philadelphia: Quaker Press of Friends General Conference, 2006.

Holton, Woody. *Black Americans in the Revolutionary Era: A Brief History with Documents.* The Bedford Series in History and Culture. Boston: Bedford/St. Martins, 2009.

Horton, James Oliver, and Lois E. Horton. *Black Bostonians: Family Life and Community Struggles in the Antebellum North.* New York: Holmes & Meier, 1979.

Jackson, John Zen. "From South Jersey Roots: The Many Facets of Dr. John S. Rock." *Salem County Historical Society Quarterly Newsletter,* 2022.

Jackson, William J. *New Jerseyans in the Civil War: For Union and Liberty.* New Brunswick, NJ: Rivergate Books, 2006.

Johnson, James Elton. "South Jersey Women of Color and the Civil War." *Vineland Historical Magazine* 90 (2019).

Jones, Jacqueline. *Labor of Love, Labor of Sorrow: Black Women, Work, and the Family, from Slavery to the Present.* New York: Vintage Books, 1986.

Kaplan, Fred. *Lincoln and the Abolitionists: John Quincy Adams, Slavery, and the Civil War.* New York: Harper Collins, 2017.

Kingseed, Wyatt. "The Fire in the Rear: Clement Vallandigham and the Copperheads." HistoryNet.com. April 11, 2016. https://www.historynet.com/the-fire-in-the-rear-clement-vallandigham-and-the-copperheads/.

Klein, Kimberly. "Princeton and the New Jersey Colonization Society." Princeton & Slavery. Accessed September 16, 2019.

Knapp, Charles Merriam. *New Jersey Politics During the Period of the Civil War and Reconstruction.* Geneva, NY: Press of W.F. Humphrey, 1924.

Kull, Irving S., ed. *New Jersey: A History.* Vol. 1. New York: American Historical Society, 1930.

Larson, Kate Clifford. *Bound for the Promised Land: Harriet Tubman, Portrait of an American Hero.* New York: Ballantine Books, 2004.

Leland, Charles Godfrey. *Abraham Lincoln and the Abolition of Slavery in the United States.* New York: Putnam's Sons, 1881.

Leonard, Elizabeth D. *All the Daring of the Soldier Women of the Civil War Armies.* New York: W.W. Norton, 1999.

Lewis, Evelyn Stryker. "Indian King Tavern." In *Encyclopedia of New Jersey,* edited by Maxine N. Lurie and Marc Mappen. New Brunswick, NJ: Rutgers University Press, 2005.

Longitude and Latitude/GPS Coordinates. "Longitude, latitude, GPS coordinates of Arlington (VA)." Accessed July 15, 2019. http://www.gps-latitude-longitude.com/gps-coordinates-of-arlington-va.

Lurie, Maxine N., ed. *A New Jersey Anthology.* New Brunswick, NJ: Rivergate Books, 2010.

Lurie, Maxine N., and Marc Mappen. *Encyclopedia of New Jersey.* New Brunswick, NJ: Rutgers University Press, 2005.

"Manumission Papers for David Cooper and Samuel Allinson." Gloucester County Slavery Book Without a Cover. Woodbury, NJ: 1774.

McCormick, Richard P. *New Jersey from Colony to State—1609–1789.* Vol. 1. Princeton: D. Van Nostrand, 1964.

McDougall, Walter S. *Throes of Democracy: The American Civil War Era 1829–1877.* New York: HarperCollins, 2008.

McGowan, James A., and William C. Kashatus. *Harriet Tubman: A Biography.* Santa Barbara, CA: Greenwood Biographies, 2011.

McMahon, William. *Historic South Jersey Towns.* Atlantic City: Press Publishing, 1964.

McManus, Edgar J. *Black Bondage in the North.* Syracuse, NY: Syracuse University Press, 1973.

McPherson, James M., ed. *The Atlas of the Civil War.* New York: Macmillan, 1994.

Measday, Walter. "Cape May and the Underground Railroad." *Cape May County New Jersey Magazine of History and Genealogy* 7, no. 3 (June 1975). Cape May County Historical and Genealogical Society.

Mickle, Isaac. *A Gentleman of Much Promise: The Diary of Isaac Mickle, 1837–1845.* Vols. 1 and 2. Edited by Philip English Mackey. Philadelphia: University of Pennsylvania Press, 1977.

Mid-Atlantic Center for the Arts. "Questions Most Often Asked about the Cape May Lighthouse." Cape May, NJ: Mid-Atlantic Center for the Arts, January 2003.

Moore, William J. "Early Negro Settlers of Cape May County." *Cape May County New Jersey Magazine of History and Genealogy* 4, no. 1 (June 1955). Cape May County Historical and Genealogical Society.

Morris, Naomi, and Julia Morris. Interview by Ellen D. Alford. Bethel Othello AME Church history interpreters. Springtown, NJ. September 6, 2014.

Mott, Lucretia Coffin. *Selected Letters of Lucretia Coffin Mott.* Edited by Beverly Wilson Palmer. Chicago: University of Illinois Press, 2002.

Mullock, Bob. Interview by Ellen D. Alford. Chairman of the board, Harriet Tubman Museum. Cape May, NJ, September 11, 2020.

Murray, Joseph Winfield, II. Interview by Ellen D. Alford. Lieutenant colonel, U.S. Army Signal Corps, retired. February 24, 2023.

Nash, Gary B. *Race and Revolution.* New York: Rowman & Littlefield, 1990.

National Archives. Hicks, John W., Age 34, Year 1864, 22nd US Colored Infantry. Carded Records Showing Military Service of Soldiers Who Fought in Volunteer Organizations During the American Civil War, 1890–1912; Records of the Adjutant General's Office 1762–1984, Record Group 94; National Archives Building, Washington, DC. Retrieved from the access to archival databases at https://www.archives.gov, January 18, 2022.

———. Tribit, William, Age 32, Year: 1864, 22nd US Colored Infantry. Carded Records Showing Military Service of Soldiers Who Fought in Volunteer Organizations During the American Civil War, 1890–1912; Records of the Adjutant General's Office 1762–1984, Record Group 94; National Archives Building, Washington, D.C. Retrieved from the access to archival databases at https://www.archives.gov, January 18, 2022.

———. *War Department General Order 143: Creation of the U.S. Colored Troops.* 1863. OurDocuments.gov.

National Archives and Records. "Compiled Military Records of United States Colored Troops 1863–1866." Washington, D.C.

National Park Service. "African Americans at the Siege of Petersburg." Petersburg National Battlefield, Richmond National Battlefield Park. Accessed August 19, 2019. https://www.nps.gov/articles/african-americans-at-the-siege-of-petersburg.htm.

———. "Andrew Jackson. The Civil War. Soldier Details." U.S. National Park Service. Retrieved from the online database at www.nps.gov, January 13, 2022.

———. "Maritime Activities." In *Southern New Jersey and the Delaware Bay.* Accessed January 25, 2021. https://www.nps.gov/parkhistory/online_books/nj2/chap3.htm#:~:text=Whaling%2chowever%2cwasundertakenwell,theonce-thrivinglocalindustry.

———. "United States Colored Troops in Opening Assaults." Accessed January 13, 2022. http://www.nps.gov/pete/learn/historyculture/united-states-colored-troops-in-opening-assaults.htm.

———. "William Tribit. The Civil War. Soldier Details." Retrieved from the online database at www.nps.gov, January 13, 2022.

New Bedford Whaling Museum. "Life Aboard." Accessed January 25, 2021. https://www.whalingmuseum.org/learn/research-topics/whaling-history/life-aboard.

———. "Yankee Whaling." Accessed January 25, 2021. https://www.whalingmuseum.org/learn/research-topics/whaling-history/yankee-whaling/.

New Jersey Colonization Society. *Proceedings of a Meeting Held at Princeton, New Jersey, July 14, 1824* […]. Princeton, NJ: D.A. Barrenstein, 1824.

New Jersey Commissioners. *Report of the Commissioners Appointed by the Legislature of New Jersey to Meet Commissioners of Virginia and Other States, at Washington, D.C., February 4.* Trenton, NJ: "True American" Office, 1861. New Jersey State Library, m/fiche JMF-0081, Cabinet K, Drawer 10, right stack.

New Jersey Writer's Project of the Works Progress Administration, ed. *Proceedings of the New Jersey State Constitutional Convention of 1844, compiled and edited by the New Jersey Writer's Project of the Work Projects Administration with an introduction by John Bedout.* Trenton: New Jersey State House Commission, 1942.

Ohio History Central. "Peace Democrats." Accessed August 19, 2019. http://www.ohiohistorycentral.org/w/Peace_Democrats.

Olden, Charles S. "Message of the Governor of New Jersey with Accompanying Documents, January 8." Trenton, NJ, 1861.

Olwell, Robert. "'Loose, Idle and Disorderly': Slave Women in the Eighteenth-Century Charleston Marketplace." In *More Than Chattel: Black Women and Slavery in the Americas*, edited by David Gasper and Darlene Clark Hine. Bloomington: Indiana University Press, 1996.

Paine, Thomas. *Common Sense and Other Writings.* Edited by Gordon S. Wood. New York: Modern Library, 2003.

Painter, Nell Irvin. *Sojourner Truth: A Life, A Symbol.* New York: W.W. Norton, 1996.

Paradis, James. *Strike the Blow: A Study of the Sixth Regiment of United States Colored Infantry.* PhD diss., Temple University, Philadelphia, 1995.

Parker, Joel. *Speech of Governor Parker, Subject: Our National Troubles—Their Causes and the Remedy.* Freehold: Campaign Document, No. 6, 1864. Library of Congress. Available at https://www.archive.org/details/speechofgovernor00park.

Pepe, Barbara. "Joshua Huddy." In *Encyclopedia of New Jersey*, edited by Maxine N. Lurie and Marc Mappen. New Brunswick, NJ: Rutgers University Press, 2005.

Perry, John Gardner. *Letters from a Surgeon of the Civil War.* Boston: Little, Brown, 1906. Available at http://www.lettersfromasur00perrygoog-civilwar-surgeon.pdf.

Peter Mott House. "A Museum of the Underground Railroad." Lawnside, NJ: 2013.

Pingeon, Frances D. *Blacks in the Revolutionary Era.* New Jersey's Revolutionary Experience 14. Trenton, NJ: New Jersey Historical Commission and the NJ American Revolution Bicentennial Celebration Commission, 1975.

Potter, David M. *The Impending Crisis 1848–1861.* Edited by Don E. Fehrenbacher. New York: Harper & Row, 1976.

Powell, Geo. R. *History of Camden County, New Jersey.* Philadelphia: L.J. Richards, 1886.

Price, Clement A., and Spencer Crew. "Abigail Goodwin." In *7 Steps to Freedom: Hear Voices from the Past Tell Tales of Freedom.* Salem: New Jersey Historical Commission, 2020.

———. "How One Woman Set Herself Free." In *7 Steps to Freedom: Hear Voices from the Past Tell Tales of Freedom.* Salem County Historical Marker, Colonel Robert Gibbons Johnson house. Salem: New Jersey Historical Commission, 2020.

———. "Poet Hetty Saunders Describes Her Escape." In *7 Steps to Freedom: Hear Voices from the Past Tell Tales of Freedom.* Salem: New Jersey Historical Commission, 2020.

———. "Thomas Clement Oliver, Underground Railroad Conductor." In *7 Steps to Freedom: Hear Voices from the Past Tell Tales of Freedom.* Salem: New Jersey Historical Commission, 2020.

Price, Clement Alexander, ed. *Freedom Not Far Distant: A Documentary History of Afro-Americans in New Jersey.* Newark: New Jersey Historical Society and the New Jersey Historical Commission, 1980.

Price, James S. *The Battle of New Market Heights Freedom Will Be Theirs by the Sword.* Edited by Douglas Bostick. Charleston, SC: The History Press, 2011.

Proprietors of West Jersey. *Concessions and Agreements of the Proprietors, Freeholders and Inhabitants of the Province of West New Jersey in America.* Mt. Holly, NJ: Herald Printing House, [1677] 1977.

The Pro-Slavery Argument; As Maintained by the Most Distinguished Writers of the Southern States, Containing the Several Essays, on the Subject, of Chancellor Harper, Governor Hammond, Dr. Simms, and Professor Dew. New York: Negro Universities Press, 1968.

Quarles, Benjamin. *The Negro in the American Revolution.* New York: W.W. Norton, 1961.

Remini, Robert V. *At the Edge of the Precipice: Henry Clay and the Compromise That Saved the Union.* New York: Basic Books, 2010.

Report of the Committee on the Conduct of the War on the Attack on Petersburg, on the 30th Day of July, 1864. Washington, D.C.: Government Printing Office, 1865.

Ricks, Mary Kay. *Escape on the Pearl: The Heroic Bid for Freedom on the Underground Railroad.* New York: William Morrow, 2007.

Russell, Henry Everett. "Negro Troops." *Continental Monthly Devoted to Literature and National Policy*, July–December 1864. University of Pennsylvania Van Pelt-Dietrick Library, Philadelphia, PA.

Salem Quarterly Meeting. *Southern New Jersey Friends and the Underground Railroad: Exploring Springtown, A Free-Black Community of Faith.* Brochure & tour, Springtown: 2014.

Salvini, Emil R. *The Summer City by the Sea: Cape May, New Jersey, An Illustrated History.* Belleville, NJ: Wheal-Grace, 1995.

Schaffer, Donald R. *After the Glory: The Struggle of Black Civil War Veterans.* Lawrence: University Press of Kansas, 2004.

Schiavo, Melissa. "Franklin Township, Gloucester County." In *Encyclopedia of New Jersey*, edited by Maxine N. Lurie and Marc Mappen. New Brunswick, NJ: Rutgers University Press, 2005.

Scott, Sr., Donald. *Camp William Penn.* Charleston, SC: Arcadia Publishing, 2008.

Scovel, Jas. M. *Three Speeches* […]. Camden, NJ: Horace B. Dick, 1870. YA Pamphlet Collection, Library of Congress. Available at http://archive.org/details/threespeeches00scov/page/n4.

Sedgwick, Theodore, Jr. *Memoir of the Life of William Livingston Member of Congress in 1774, 1775, and 1776* [...]. New York: J&J Harper, 1833.

Seward House. *Seward House: Meet An American Hero.* Brochure & tour. Auburn, NY: Seward House.

Siebert, Wilbur H. *The Underground Railroad from Slavery to Freedom.* New York: Russell & Russell, [1898] 1967.

Simpson, Hazel B., ed. *Under Four Flags Old Gloucester County 1686–1964: A History of Gloucester, County New Jersey.* Camden, NJ: Sinnickson Chew & Sons, 1965.

Sizer, Lyde Cullen. "Acting Her Part: Narratives of Union Women Spies." In *Divided Houses: Gender and the Civil War*, edited by Catherine Clinton and Nina Silber. New York: Oxford University Press, 1992.

Skinner, William H. *Black Civil War Soldiers from the Counties of Camden, Cumberland, Gloucester and Salem, N.J.* Report, Gloucester County Historical Society, Woodbury, 1993.

Smedley, R.C. *The American Negro His History and Literature History of the Underground Railroad.* New York: Arno Press and the *New York Times*, 1969.

Stellhorn, Paul A., ed. "Political Oligarch, Egalitarianism and Continuity in New Jersey: 1840–1860." In *Jacksonian New Jersey*, by Philip C. Davis. Trenton, NJ: New Jersey Historical Commission, 1979.

Stevens, Lewis Townsend. *The History of Cape May County New Jersey From the Abioriginal Times to the Present Day.* Cape May City, NJ: Press of the Star of the Cape, 1897.

Still, William. *The Underground Railroad, A Record of Facts, Authentic Narratives, Letters, & c* […]. Medford, NJ: Plexus, [1872] 2005.

Swedesboro Economic Development Committee. *Stroll Through "Mortenson-Van Leer Log Cabin (c.1640's)," and "Mount Zion AME Church and Mount Zion Cemetery."* Stroll through Swedesboro, NJ: Take Our Walking Tour. Brochure. Swedesboro, NJ: Swedesboro Economic Development Committee.

Swisher, Carl B. *The Oliver Wendell Holmes Devise. History of the Supreme Court of the United States: The Taney Period 1836–64.* Edited by Paul A. Freund. Vol. 5. New York: Macmillan, 1974.

Taggart, John H. *Free Military School for Applicants for Command of Colored Troops.* Supervisory Committee for Recruiting Colored Regiments. Philadelphia: King & Baird, 1863. The Union League Library, Philadelphia, PA.

Taylor, Frank H. *Philadelphia in the Civil War 1861–1865.* Philadelphia: City of Philadelphia, 1913.

Taylor, William R. *Cavalier and Yankee: The Old South and American National Character.* New York: George Braziller, 1961.

Tobin, Jacqueline L., and Raymond G. Dobard. *Hidden in Plain View: A Secret Story of Quilts and the Underground Railroad.* New York: Anchor Books, 2000.

"Township of Franklin Residents Serving in the American Civil War 1861–1865." Veterans' Register (notebook). Betty Basjewicz Historical Center, Franklinville, NJ.

Towns, Lynda. Interview by Ellen D. Alford. President, Harriet Tubman Museum. Cape May, NJ. September 11, 2020.

Trevelyan, George Otto. *The American Revolution Part III Saratoga and Brandywine Valley Forge England and France at War.* Vol. 3. New York: Longmans, Green, 1909.

Trudeau, Noah Andre. *Like Men of War: Black Troops in the Civil War 1862–1865.* Boston: Little, Brown, 1998.

U.S. Bureau of the Census. U.S. Census, 1800–60. Washington, D.C.: U.S. Government.

———. U.S. Census, 1860. Franklin Township. Gloucester County, N.J. Washington, D.C.: Government Printing Office. New Jersey State Library, Trenton, NJ. Microfilm, 1845–1860, Micro Copy No. M653, Roll No. 691, Cabinet A, Drawer 9.

———. U.S. Census. 1860. State of New Jersey. Population by Color and Condition. Table No. 2. Washington, D.C.: U.S. Government.

"War Department General Order 143: Creation of the U.S. Colored Troops (1863)." 1863. OurDocuments.gov.

Ward, Samuel Ringgold. *Autobiography of a Fugitive Negro: His Anti-Slavery Labors in the United States, Canada, & England.* Chicago: Ebony Classics Johnson, 1970.

Washington, Ethel M. *Union County's Black Soldiers and Sailors of the Civil War.* Charleston, SC: The History Press, 2011.

West Cape May Citizens for Good Government. "Architectural & Historic Features." Cape Island, NJ car free/care free biking, hinking, birding map. Cape May, NJ: West Cape May Citizens for Good Government, 2004.

White, Deborah Gray. *Ar'n't I a Woman? Female Slaves in the Plantation South.* New York: W.W. Norton, 1999.

Whittaker, Celeste E. "S.J. Had Many Stops on the Underground Railroad." *Daily Journal,* February 19, 2002.

Wilson, Harold F. *The Story of the Jersey Shore.* Vol. 4. Princeton, NJ: D. Van Nostrand, 1964.

Wilson, Joseph T. *The Black Phalanx: A History of the Negro Soldiers of the United States in the Wars of 1775–1812, 1861–'65.* Hartford, CT: American Publishing, 1888.

Wolinetz, Gary K. "New Jersey Slavery and the Law." *Rutgers Law Review* 50, no. 4 (Summer 1998): 2254–55.

Woodson, C.G. *The Education of the Negro Prior to 1861: A History of the Education of the Colored People of the United States from the Beginning of Slavery to the Civil War.* 2nd ed. Washington, D.C.: Associated Publishers, 1919.

Woolman, John. *Journal of the Life, Gospel Labours, and Christian Experiences of That Faithful Minister of Jesus Christ, John Woolman, Late of Mount Holly, in the Province of New Jersey.* Philadelphia: Friends' Book Association, 1892.

Wright, Giles R. *Afro-Americans in New Jersey: A Short History.* Trenton: New Jersey Commission, Department of State, 1988.

———. *Moving Toward Breaking the Chains: Black Jerseyans and the American Revolution.* 2nd ed. Edited by Maxine N. Lurie. New Brunswick, NJ: Rivergate Books, 2010.

Wright, Marion M. Thompson. *The Education of Negroes in New Jersey.* New York: Arno Press & the *New York Times*, 1971.

Zilversmit, Arthur. *The First Emancipation: The Abolition of Slavery in the North.* Chicago: University of Chicago Press, 1967.

ABOUT THE AUTHOR

Ellen D. Alford is a native South Jersey resident and local historian who researches and writes about the Underground Railroad, slavery, abolition and Harriet Tubman in South Jersey. She is a former newspaper correspondent, public school educator and college/university administrator. Alford has published articles in the *Vineland Historical Magazine* and the *Bulletin* of the Gloucester County Historical Society. In 2011, she presented a paper to the Mid-Atlantic Popular/American Culture Association's Twenty-Second Annual Conference in Philadelphia, Pennsylvania. She has won the Lloyd P. Burns Award for Public Service from the New Jersey Press Association; First Place for Spot News from Sigma Delta Chi Association, Philadelphia chapter; First Place for Spot News from the New Jersey Press Association; and an honorable mention from the Philadelphia Press Association for Spot News.

Alford is a graduate of Howard University in Washington, D.C., with a degree in English/communications and has pursued graduate studies in American history at Rutgers University in Camden, New Jersey, where she was awarded the A&S Academic Excellence Award. Alford is a member of the National History Honor Society.

Visit us at
www.historypress.com